Charles P. Otis

Voyages of Samuel de Champlain v.3

Charles P. Otis

Voyages of Samuel de Champlain v.3

ISBN/EAN: 9783742840752

Manufactured in Europe, USA, Canada, Australia, Japa

Cover: Foto ©Thomas Meinert / pixelio.de

Manufactured and distributed by brebook publishing software
(www.brebook.com)

Charles P. Otis

Voyages of Samuel de Champlain v.3

.

THE

Publications of the Prince Society.

Established May 25th, 1858.

CHAMPLAIN'S VOYAGES.

Boston:
PRINTED FOR THE SOCIETY,
BY JOHN WILSON AND SON.
1882.

VOYAGES

OF

SAMUEL DE CHAMPLAIN.

TRANSLATED FROM THE FRENCH

BY CHARLES POMEROY OTIS, PH.D.

WITH HISTORICAL ILLUSTRATIONS,

AND A

MEMOIR

BY THE REV. EDMUND F. SLAFTER, A.M.

VOL. III.

1611–1618.

HELIOTYPE COPIES OF TEN MAPS AND ILLUSTRATIONS.

Boston:

PUBLISHED BY THE PRINCE SOCIETY.

1882.

Editor :

THE REV. EDMUND F. SLAFTER, A.M.

PREFACE.

THE prefent volume completes the work propofed by the Prince Society of a tranflation into Eng-lifh of the VOYAGES OF CHAMPLAIN. It includes the journals iffued in 1604, 1613, and 1619, and covers fifteen years of his refidence and explorations in New France.

At a later period, in 1632, Champlain publifhed, in a fingle volume, an abridgment of the iffues above mentioned, containing likewife a continuation of his journal down to 1631. This continuation covers thirteen additional years. But it is to be obferved that the events recorded in the journal of thefe later years are immediately connected with the progrefs and local interefts of the French colony at Quebec. This laft work of the great explorer is of primary importance and value as conftituting original material for the early hiftory of Canada, and a tranflation of it into Englifh would doubt-lefs be highly appreciated by the local hiftorian. A complete narrative of thefe events, however, together with a large

amount

amount of interesting matter relating to the career of Champlain derived from other sources, is given in the Memoir contained in the first volume of this work.

This Englifh tranflation contains not only the complete narratives of all the perfonal explorations made by Champlain into the then unbroken forefts of America, but the whole of his minute, ample, and invaluable defcriptions of the character and habits, mental, moral, and phyfical, of the various favage tribes with which he came in contact. It will furnifh, therefore, to the ftudent of hiftory and the ftudent of ethnology moft valuable information, unfurpaffed in richnefs and extent, and which cannot be obtained from any other fource. To aid one or both of thefe two claffes in their inveftigations, the work was undertaken and has now been completed.

E. F. S.

Boston, 91 Boylston Street,
April 5, 1882.

TABLE OF CONTENTS.

ILLUSTRATIONS.

THE VOYAGES

OF SIEUR DE CHAMPLAIN,

Of Saintonge, Captain in ordinary to the
King in the Marine;

OR,

*A MOST FAITHFUL JOURNAL OF OBSERVATIONS
made in the exploration of New France, describing not only the
countries, coasts, rivers, ports, and harbors, with their latitudes,
and the various deflections of the Magnetic Needle, but likewise the
religious belief of the inhabitants, their superstitions, mode of life
and warfare; furnished with numerous illustrations.*

Together with two geographical maps: the first for the purposes of
navigation, adapted to the compass as used by mariners, which
deflects to the north-east; the other in its true meridian, with
longitudes and latitudes, to which is added the Voyage to the
Strait north of Labrador, from the 53d to the 63d degree of latitude, discovered in 1612 by the English when they were searching
for a northerly course to China.

PARIS.

JEAN BERJON, Rue St. Jean de Beauvais, at the Flying Horse,
and at his store in the Palace, at the gallery
of the Prisoners.

M. DC. XIII.

WITH AUTHORITY OF THE KING.

THIRD VOYAGE

OF

SIEUR DE CHAMPLAIN,

IN THE YEAR 1611.

CHAPTER I.

DEPARTURE FROM FRANCE TO RETURN TO NEW FRANCE. — THE DANGERS
AND OTHER EVENTS WHICH OCCURRED UP TO THE TIME OF ARRIVAL AT
THE SETTLEMENT.

E fet out from Honfleur on the firſt day of March.
The wind was favorable until the eighth, when
we were oppofed by a wind fouth-fouthweſt and
weſt-northweſt, driving us as far as latitude 42°,
without our being able to make a fouthing, fo
as to fail ſtraight forward on our courfe. Accordingly
after encountering feveral heavy winds, and being kept back
by bad weather, we neverthelefs, through great difficulty and
hardſhip, and by failing on different tacks, fucceeded in arriving within eighty leagues of the Grand Bank, where the
freſh fiſhery is carried on. Here we encountered ice thirty
or forty fathoms high, or more, which led us to confider
what courfe we ought to take, fearing that we might fall in

1   with

with more during the night, or that the wind changing would
drive us on to it. We also concluded that this would not be
the last, since we had set out from France too early in the season. We failed **accordingly** during that day with short sail,
as near the wind as we could. When night came, the fog
arose so **thick** and obscure that we could scarcely see the
ship's length. About eleven o'clock at night, more ice was
seen, which alarmed us. But through the energy of the sailors we avoided it. Supposing that we had passed all danger,
we met with still more ice, which the sailors saw ahead of our
vessel, but not until we were almost upon it. When all had
committed themselves to God, having given up all hope of
avoiding collision with this ice, which was already under our
bowsprit, they cried to the helmsman to bear off; and this ice
which was very extensive drove in such a manner that it passed
by without striking our vessel, which stopped short, and remained as still as if it had never moved, to let it pass. Although
the danger was over, our blood was not so quickly cooled, so
great had been our fear, and we praised God for delivering
us from so imminent a peril. This experience being over, we
passed the same night two or three other masses of ice, not
less dangerous than the former ones. There was at the same
time a dripping fog, and it was so cold that we could scarcely
get warm. The next day we met several other large and
very high masses of ice, which, in the distance, looked like
islands. We, however, avoided them all, and reached the
Grand Bank, where we were detained by bad weather for the
space of six days. The wind growing a little milder, and
very favorable, we left the banks in latitude 44° 30′, which
was the farthest south we could go. After sailing some sixty
leagues

leagues weft-northweft, we faw a veffel coming down to **make** us out, but which afterwards wore off to the eaft-northeaft, to avoid a large bank of ice, which covered the entire extent of our line of vifion. Concluding that there was a paffage through the middle of this great floe, which was divided into two parts, we entered, in purfuance of our courfe, between **the** two, and failed fome ten leagues without feeing anything, contrary to our conjecture of a fine paffage through, until evening, when we found the floe clofed up. This gave **us** much anxiety as to what was to be done, the night being at hand and there being no moon, which deprived us of all means of returning to the point whence we had come. Yet, after due deliberation, it was refolved to try to find again the entrance by which we had come, which we fet about accomplifhing. But the night coming on with fog, rain, fnow, and a wind fo violent that we could fcarcely carry our mainfail, **every** trace of our way was loft. For, as we were expecting **to avoid** the ice fo as to pafs out, the wind had already clofed up **the** paffage, fo that we were obliged to return to the other tack. We were unable to remain longer than a quarter of an hour on one tack before taking another, in order to avoid the numerous maffes of ice drifting about on all fides. We thought more than twenty times that we should never efcape with our lives. The entire night was fpent amid difficulties and hardfhips. Never was the watch better kept, for nobody wifhed to reft, but to ftrive to efcape from the ice and danger. The cold was fo great, that all the ropes of the veffel were fo frozen and covered with large icicles that the men could not work her nor ftick to the deck. Thus we ran, on this tack and that, awaiting with hope the daylight.

light. But when it came, attended by a fog, and we faw that our labor and hardfhip could not avail us anything, we determined to go to a mafs of ice, where we fhould be fheltered from the violent wind which was blowing ; to haul everything down, and allow ourfelves to be driven along with the ice, fo that when at fome diftance from the reft of the ice we could make fail again, and go back to the above-mentioned bank and manage as before, until the fog fhould pafs away, when we might go out as quickly as poffible. Thus we continued the entire day until the morning of the next day, when we fet fail, now on this tack now on that, finding ourfelves everywhere enclofed amid large floes of ice, as if in lakes on the mainland. At evening we fighted a veffel on the other fide of one of thefe banks of ice, which, I am fure, was **in no lefs** anxiety than ourfelves. Thus we remained four or five days, expofed to thefe rifks and extreme hardfhips, until one morning on looking out in all directions, although we could fee no opening, yet in one place it feemed as if the ice was not thick, and that we could eafily pafs through. We got under weigh, and paffed by a large number of *bourguignons ;* that is, pieces of ice feparated from the large banks by the violence of the winds. Having reached this bank of ice, the failors proceeded to provide themfelves with large oars and pieces of wood, in order to keep off the blocks of ice we met. In this way we paffed this bank, but not without touching fome pieces of ice, which did no good to our veffel, although they inflicted no effential damage. Being outfide, we praifed God for our deliverance. Continuing our courfe on the next day, we encountered other pieces, in which we became fo involved that we found ourfelves furrounded

rounded on all fides, except where we had entered. It was
accordingly neceffary to turn back, and endeavor to double
the fouthern point. This we did not fucceed in doing until
the fecond day, paffing by feveral fmall pieces of ice, which
had been feparated from the main bank. This latter was in
latitude 44° 30'. We failed until the morning of the next
day, towards the northweft, north-northweft, when we met
another large ice bank, extending as far as we could fee eaft
and weft. This, in the diftance, feemed like land, for it was
fo level that it might properly be faid to have been made fo
on purpofe. It was more than eighteen feet high, extending
twice as far under water. We calculated that we were only
fome fifteen leagues from Cape Breton, it being the 26th
day of the month. Thefe numerous encounters with ice
troubled us greatly. We were alfo fearful that the paffage
between Capes Breton and Raye would be clofed, and that
we fhould be obliged to keep out to fea a long time before
being able to enter. Unable to do anything elfe, we were
obliged to run out to fea again fome four or five leagues, in
order to double another point of the above-mentioned grand
ice bank, which continued on our weft-fouthweft. After
turning on the other tack to the northweft, in order to double
this point, we failed fome feven leagues, and then fteered to
the north-northweft fome three leagues, when we obferved
another ice bank. The night approached, and the fog came
on fo that we put to fea to pafs the remainder of the night,
purpofing at daybreak to return and reconnoitre the laft
mentioned ice. On the twenty-feventh day of the month, we
fighted land weft-northweft of us, feeing no ice on the north-
northeaft. We approached nearer for the fake of a better
                                                    obfervation,

obfervation, and found that it was Canfeau. This led us to
bear off to the north for Cape Breton Ifland; but we had
fcarcely failed two leagues when we encountered an ice bank
on the northeaft. Night coming on, we were obliged to put
out to fea until the next day, when we failed northeaft, and
encountered more ice, bearing eaft, eaft-southeaft from us,
along which we coafted heading northeaft and north for
more than fifteen leagues. At laft we were obliged to fail
towards the weft, greatly to our regret, inafmuch as we could
find no paffage, and fhould be obliged to withdraw and fail
back on our track. Unfortunately for us we were overtaken
by **a calm,** fo that it feemed as if the fwell of the fea would
throw us upon the ice bank juft mentioned, and we got
ready to launch our little boat, to ufe in cafe of neceffity.
If we had taken refuge on the above-mentioned ice it would
only have been to languifh and die in mifery. While we
were deliberating whether to launch our boat, a frefh breeze
arofe to our great delight, and thus we efcaped from the ice.
After we had failed two leagues, night came on, with a very
thick fog, caufing us to haul down our fail, as we could not
fee, and as there were feveral large pieces of ice in our way,
which we were afraid of ftriking. Thus we remained the
entire night until the next day, which was the twenty-ninth,
when the fog increafed to fuch an extent that we could
fcarcely fee the length of the veffel. There was alfo very
little wind. Yet we did not fail to fet fail, in order to avoid
the ice. But, although expecting to extricate ourfelves, we
found ourfelves fo involved in it that we could not tell on
which fide to tack. We were accordingly again compelled
to lower fail, and drift until the ice fhould allow us to make
fail.

fail. We made a hundred tacks on one fide and the other, feveral times fearing that we were loft. The moft felf-pof-feffed would have loft all judgment in fuch a juncture; even the greateft navigator in the world. What alarmed us ftill more was the fhort diftance we could fee, and the fact that the night was coming on, and that we could not make a fhift of a quarter of a league without finding a bank or fome ice, and a great deal of floating ice, the fmalleft piece of which would have been fufficient to caufe the lofs of any veffel **whatever.** Now, while we were ftill failing along amid the **ice, there arofe** fo ftrong a wind that in a fhort time the fog broke away, affording us a view, and fuddenly giving us a clear air and fair fun. Looking around about us, we found that we were fhut up in a little lake, not fo much as a league and a half in circuit. On the north we perceived the ifland of Cape Breton, nearly four leagues diftant, and it feemed to us that the paffage-way to Cape Breton was ftill clofed. We **alfo faw a** fmall ice bank aftern of our veffel, and the ocean beyond that, which led us to refolve to go beyond the bank, which was divided. This we fucceeded in accomplifhing with-out ftriking our veffel, putting out to fea for the night, and paffing to the foutheaft of the ice. Thinking now that we could double this ice bank, we failed eaft-northeaft fome fifteen leagues, perceiving only a little piece of ice. At night we hauled down the fail until the next day, when we perceived another ice bank to the north of us, extending as far as we could fee. We had drifted to within nearly half a league of it, when we hoifted fail, continuing to coaft along this ice in order to find the end of it. While failing along, we fighted on the firft day of May a veffel amid the ice, which,

as well as ourfelves, had found it difficult to efcape from it.
We backed our fails in order to await the former, which
came full upon us, fince we were defirous of afcertaining
whether it had feen other ice.   On its approach we faw that
it **was the fon**[1] **of** Sieur de Poutrincourt, on his way to vifit
his father at **the** fettlement of Port Royal.   He had left
France three months before, not without much reluctance, I
think, and ftill they were nearly a hundred and forty leagues
from Port Royal, and well out of their true courfe.   We told
them we had fighted the iflands of Canfeau, much to their
fatisfaction, I think, as they had not as yet fighted any land,
and were fleering ftraight between Cape St. Lawrence and
Cape Raye, in which direction they would not have found
Port Royal, except by going overland.   After a brief confer-
ence with each other we feparated, each following his own
courfe.   The next day we fighted the iflands of St. Pierre,
finding no ice.   Continuing our courfe we fighted on the following day, the third of the month, Cape Raye, alfo without
finding ice.   On the fourth we fighted the ifland of St. Paul,
and Cape St. Lawrence, being fome eight leagues north of
the latter.   The next day we fighted Gafpé.   On the feventh
we were oppofed by a northweft wind, which drove us out of
our courfe nearly thirty-five leagues, when the wind lulled,
and was in our favor as far as Tadouffac, which we reached
on the 13th day of May.[2]   Here we difcharged a cannon to
notify the favages, in order to obtain news from our fettlement

[1] This was Charles de Biencourt,
Sieur de Saint Juft.   He was clofely
affociated with his father, Sieur de
Poutrincourt, in his colony at Port
Royal.   *Vide* Vol. I. p. 122, note 77.

[2] They left Honfleur on the firft day
of March, and were thus feventy-four
days in reaching Tadouffac.   The voyage was ufually made in favorable
weather in thirty days.

ment at Quebec. The country was still almost entirely covered with snow. There came out to us some canoes, informing us that one of our pataches had been in the harbor for a month, and that three veffels had arrived eight days before. We lowered our boat and vifited thefe favages, who were in a very miferable condition, having only a few articles to barter to fatisfy their immediate wants. Befides they defired to wait until feveral veffels fhould meet, fo that there might be a better market for their **merchandife**. Therefore they are miftaken who expect to gain **an** advantage by coming firft, for thefe people are very fagacious and cunning.

On the 17th of the month I fet out from Tadouffac for the great fall,[3] to meet the Algonquin favages and other tribes, who had promifed the year before to go there with my man, whom I had fent to them, that I might learn from him what he might fee during the winter. Thofe at this harbor who fufpected where I was going, in accordance with the promifes which I had made to the favages, as ftated above, began to build feveral fmall barques, that they might follow me as foon as poffible. And feveral, as I learned before fetting out from France, had fome fhips and pataches fitted out in view of our voyage, hoping to return rich, as from a voyage to the Indies.

Pont Gravé remained at **Tadouffac expecting, if he did** nothing there, to take **a patache and meet me at the fall.** Between Tadouffac and Quebec **our** barque made much water, which obliged me to ftop at Quebec and repair the leak. This was on the 21ft day of May. CHAPTER II.

[3] The Falls of St. Louis, near Montreal, now more commonly known as the La Chine Rapids.

CHAPTER II.

Landing at Quebec to repair the Barque. — Departure from Quebec for the Fall, to meet the Savages, and search out a Place appropriate for a Settlement.

ON going ashore I found Sieur du Parc, who had spent the winter at the settlement. **He and all** his companions were **very well, and had not** suffered any sicknefs. Game, both large **and** small, had been abundant during the entire winter, **as they** told me. I found there the Indian captain, named *Batifcan*, and some Algonquins, who said they were **waiting for** me, being unwilling to return to Tadousfac without **feeing me.** I propofed to them to take one of our com**pany to** the *Trois Rivières* to explore the place, but being **unable to** obtain anything from them this year I put it off until the next. Still I did not fail to inform myfelf particularly regarding the origin of the people living there, of which they told me with exactnefs. I afked them for one of their canoes, which they were unwilling to part with on any terms, becaufe of their own need of it. For I had planned to fend two or three men to explore the neighborhood of the **Trois** Rivières, and afcertain what there was there. This, to my great regret, I was unable to accomplifh, and postponed the project to the firft opportunity that might prefent itfelf.

Meanwhile I urged on the repairs to our barque. When it was ready, a young man from La Rochelle, named Trefart, afked me to permit him to accompany me to the above-
mentioned

mentioned fall. This I refufed, replying that I had **fpecial** plans of my own, and that I did not wifh to conduct any one to my prejudice, adding that there were other companies than mine there, and that I did not care to open up a way and ferve as guide, and that he could make the voyage well enough alone and without my help.

The fame day I fet out from Quebec, and arrived at the great fall on the twenty-eighth of May. But I found none of the favages who had promifed me to be there on this **day. I entered at** once a poor canoe, together with the fav-age I had taken to France and one of my own men. After examining the two fhores, both in the woods and on the river bank, in order to find a fpot favorable for the location of a fettlement, and to get a place ready for building, I went fome eight leagues by land along the great fall and through the woods, which are very open, as far as a lake,[4] whither our favage conducted me. Here I obferved the country very **carefully.** But in all that I faw, I found no place more **favorable** than a little fpot to which barques and fhallops can eafily afcend, with the help of a ftrong wind or by taking a winding courfe, in confequence of the ftrong current. But above this place, which we named *La Place Royale*, at the diftance of a league from Mont Royal, there are a great many little rocks and fhoals, which are very dangerous. Near Place Royale there is a little river, extending fome diftance into the interior, along the entire length of which there are more than fixty acres of land cleared up and like meadows, where grain can be fown and gardens made. Formerly

[4] This journey of eight leagues would take them as far as the Lake of Two Mountains.

merly favages tilled thefe lands,[b] but they abandoned them on account of their wars, in which they were conftantly engaged. There **is** alfo a large number of other fine paftures, where **any** number of cattle can graze. There are alfo the various **kinds of trees** found in France, together with many vines, nut and plum trees, cherries, ftrawberries, and other kinds of good fruit. Among the reft there is a very excellent one, with a fweet tafte like that of plantains, a fruit of the Indies, as white as fnow, with a leaf refembling that of nettles, and which

[b] This little river is mentioned by Champlain in his Voyage of 1603, Vol. I. p. 268. It is reprefented on early maps as formed by two fmall ftreams, flowing, one from the north or northeaftern, and the other from the fouthern fide of the mountain, in the **rear** of the city of Montreal, which unite fome diftance before they reach the St. Lawrence, flowing into that river at Point Callières. Thefe little brooks are laid down on Champlain's local map, *Le Grand Sault St. Louis*, on Charlevoix's *Carte de l'Ifle de Montréal*, 1744, and on Bellin's *L'Ifle de Montréal*, 1764; but they have difappeared on modern maps, and probably are either extinct or are loft in the fewerage of the city, of which they have become a part. We have called the ftream formed by thefe two brooks, note 190, Vol. I., *Rivière St. Pierre*. On Potherie's map, the only ftream coming from the interior is fo named. *Vide Hiftoire de L'Amérique* par M. de Bacqueville de la Potherie, 1722, p. 311. On a map in Greig's *Hocheloga Depicta*, 1839, it is called St. Peter's River. The fame ftream on Bouchette's map, 1831, is denominated Little River. It feems not unlikely that a part of it was called, at one time,

Rivière St. Pierre, and another **part** Petite Rivière.

It is plain that on this ftream was fituated the fixty acres of cleared land alluded to in the text as formerly occupied by the favages.

It will be remembered that feventy-fix years anterior to this, in 1535, Jacques Cartier difcovered this place, which was then the feat of a large and flourifhing Indian town. It is to be regretted that Champlain did not inform us more definitely as to the hiftory of the former occupants of the foil. Some important, and we think conclufive, reafons have been affigned for fuppofing that they were a tribe of the Iroquois. Among others may be mentioned the fimilarity in the conftruction of their towns and houfes or cabins, the identity of their language as determined by a collation of the words found in Cartier's journal with the language of the Iroquois; and to thefe may be added the traditions obtained by miffionaries and others, as cited by Laverdière, to which we muft not, however, attach too much value. *Vide Laverdière in loco.* While it feems probable that the former occupants were of the Iroquois family, it is impoffible to determine whether on retiring they **joined**

which creeps up the trees and along the ground like ivy.[6]
Fish are very abundant, including all the varieties we have in
France, and many very good ones which we do not have.
Game is also plenty, the birds being of various kinds. There
are stags, hinds, does, caribous,[7] rabbits, lynxes,[8] bears, beavers, also other small animals, and all in such large numbers,
that while we were at the fall we were abundantly supplied
with them.

After a careful examination, we found this place one of
the finest on this river. I accordingly forthwith gave orders
to cut down and clear up the woods in the Place Royale,[9]

so

joined the Five Nations in the State of
New York, or merged themselves with
the Hurons, who were likewise of Iroquois origin.

[6] I am unable to identify this plant.
Its climbing propensity and the color of
its fruit suggest *Rhus radicans*, but in
other respects the similarity fails.

[7] *Cerfs, Daims, Chevreuils, Caribous.*
Champlain employs the names of the
different species of the Cerf family as
used in Europe; but as our species are
different, this use of names creates
some confusion. There were in Canada,
the moose, the caribou, the wapiti, and
the common red deer. Any enumera-
tion by the early writers must include
these, under whatever names they may
be described. One will be found ap-
plying a name to a given species, while
another will apply the same name to
quite a different species. Charlevoix
mentions the original (moose) caribou,
the hart, and the roebuck. Under the
name *hart*, he probably refers to the
wapiti, *elaphus Canadensis*, and roebuck, to the common red deer, *Cervus
Virginianus*. *Vide Charlevoix's Letters to the Dutchess of Lesdiguieres*,

1763, pp. 64-69, also Vol. I. of this
work, p. 265.

[8] Lynxes, *Loups-cerviers*. The com-
pound word *loup-cervier* was significant,
and was applied originally to the animal
of which the stag was its natural prey,
qui attaque les cerfs. In Europe it
described the lynx, a large powerful animal of the feline race, that might well
venture to attack the stag. But in
Canada this species is not found. What
is known as the Canadian lynx, *Felis
Canadensis*, is only a large species of
cat, which preys upon birds and the
smaller quadrupeds. Champlain probably gives it the name *loup-cervier* for
the want of one more appropriate. It
is a little remarkable that he does not
in this list mention the American wolf,
Lupus occidentalis, so common in
every part of Canada, and which he
subsequently refers to as the animal
especially dreaded by the deer. *Vide
Aydea*, pp. 139, 157.

[9] The site of Place Royale was on
Point Callières, so named in honor of
Chevalier Louis Hector de Callières
Bonnevue, governor of Montreal in
1684.

so as to level it and prepare it for building. The water can easily be made to flow around it, making of it a little island, so that a habitation can be formed as one may wish.

There is a little island some twenty fathoms from Place Royale, about **a** hundred paces long, where a good and strong settlement might be made. There are also many meadows, containing very good and rich potter's clay, as well adapted for brick as for building purposes, and consequently a very useful article. I had a portion of it worked up, from which I made a wall four feet thick, three or four high, and ten fathoms long, to see how it would stand during the winter, when the freshets came down, although I thought the water would not reach up to it, the ground there being twelve feet above the river, which was very high. In the middle of the river there was an island about three-quarters of a league around, where a good and strong town could be built. This we named *Isle de Sainte Hélène.*[20] This river at the fall is like a lake, containing two or three islands, and bordered by fine meadows.

On the first day of June, Pont Gravé arrived at the fall, having been unable to accomplish anything at Tadoussac. A numerous company attended and followed after him to share in the booty, without the hope of which they would have been far in the rear.

Now, while awaiting the savages, I had two gardens made, one in the meadows, the other in the woods, which I had cleared up. On the 2d of June I sowed some seeds, all of

which

[20] It seems most likely that the name of this island was suggested by the marriage which Champlain had contracted with Hélène Boullé, the year before. This name had been given to several other places. *Vide* Vol. I. pp. 104, 105.

which came up finely, and in a fhort time, attefting the good quality of the foil.

We refolved to fend Savignon, our favage, together with another, to meet his countrymen, fo as to haften their arrival. They hefitated about going in our canoe, of which they were diftruftful, it being a very poor one. They fet out on the 5th. The next day four or five barques arrived as an efcort for us, fince they could do nothing at Tadouffac.

On the 7th I went to explore a little river, along which the favages fometimes go to war, and which flows into the fall of the river of the Iroquois.[11] It is very pleafant, with meadow land more than three leagues in circuit, and much arable land. It is diftant a league from the great fall, and a league and a half from Place Royale.

On the 9th our favage arrived. He had gone fomewhat beyond the lake, which is ten leagues long, and which I had feen before.[12] But he met no one, and they were unable to go any farther, as their canoe gave out, which obliged them **to** return. They reported that after paffing the fall they faw an ifland, where there was fuch a quantity of herons that the air was completely filled with them. There was a young man belonging to Sieur de Monts named Louis, who was very fond of the chafe. Hearing this, he wifhed to go and fatisfy his curiofity, earneftly entreating our favage to take him to the place. To this the favage confented, taking alfo a captain of the Montagnais, a very refpectable perfon, whofe name was *Outetoucos.* On the following morning Louis caufed the two favages to be called, and went with them

[11] *Vide* Vol. I. p. 268, note 191. *Walker and Miles's Atlas,* map 186.   [12] The Lake of the Two Mountains. *Vide antea,* note 4.

them in a canoe to the iſland of the herons.   This iſland is in
the middle of the fall.[13]   Here they captured as many herons
and other **birds as** they wanted, and embarked again in their
canoe.   Outetoucos, contrary to the wiſh of the other ſavage,
and againſt his remonſtrances, deſired to paſs through a very
dangerous place, where the water fell more than three feet,
ſaying that he had formerly gone this way, which, however,
was falſe.   He had a long diſcuſſion in oppoſition to our
ſavage, who wiſhed to take him on the ſouth ſide, along the
mainland,[14] where they uſually go.   This, however, Outetoucos did not wiſh, ſaying that there was no danger.   Our
ſavage finding him obſtinate yielded to his deſire.   But he
inſiſted **that at** leaſt a part of the birds in the canoe ſhould
be **taken** out, as it was overloaded, otherwiſe he ſaid it
would inevitably fill and be loſt.   But to this he would not
conſent, ſaying that it would be time enough when they found
themſelves in the preſence of danger.   They accordingly
permitted themſelves to be carried along by the current.
But when they reached the precipice, they wanted to throw
overboard their load in order to eſcape.   It was now, however, too late, for they were completely in the power of
the rapid water, and were ſtraightway ſwallowed up in the
whirlpools of the fall, which turned them round a thouſand
times.   For a long time they clung to the boat.   Finally the
ſwiftneſs of the water wearied them ſo that this poor Louis,
who

---

[13] On Champlain's local map of the
Falls of St. Louis, the letter Q is wanting ; but the expreſſion, *ceſte iſle eſt au
milieu du ſaut,* " in the middle of the
fall," as ſuggeſted by Laverdière, in-
dicates that the iſland deſignated by

the letter R is Heron Iſland.   *Vide
poſtea,* R on map at p. 18.

[14] *Grand Tibie,* ſo in the original.
This is a typographical error for *grand
terre.   Vide* Champlain, 1632, Quebec
ed., p. 842.

who could not fwim at all, entirely loft his prefence of mind, and, the canoe going down, he was obliged to abandon it. As it returned to the furface, the two others who kept holding on to it, faw Louis no more, and thus he died a fad death.[18] The two others continued to hold on to the canoe. When, however, they were out of danger, this Outetoucos, being naked and having confidence in his fwimming powers, abandoned it in the expectation of reaching **the** fhore, although the water ftill ran there with great rapidity. But he was drowned, for he had been fo weakened and overcome by his efforts that it was impoffible for him to fave himfelf after abandoning the canoe. Our favage Savignon, underftanding himfelf better, held firmly to the canoe until it reached an eddy, whither the current had carried it. Here he managed fo well that, notwithftanding his fuffering and wearinefs, he approached the fhore gradually, when, after throwing the water out of the canoe, he returned in great fear that they **would** take vengeance upon him, as the favages do among themfelves, and related to us this fad ftory, which caufed us great forrow.

On the next day I went in another canoe to the fall, together with the favage and another member of our company, to fee the place where they had met with their accident, and find, if poffible, the remains. But when he fhowed me the fpot, I was horrified at beholding fuch a terrible place, and aftonifhed that the deceafed fhould have been

[18] The death of this young man may have fuggefted the name which was afterward given to the fall. He was, however, it is reafonable to fuppofe, hardly equal in fanctity of character to the Saint Louis of the French. Hitherto it had been called *Le Grand Saut.* But foon after this it began to be called *Grand Saut S. Louys. Vide poftea*, pp. 38, 51, 59.

been fo lacking in judgment as to pafs through fuch a fearful place, when they could have gone another way. For it
is impoffible to go along there, as there are feven or eight
defcents of water one after the other, the loweft three feet
high, the feething and boiling of the water being fearful. A
part of the fall was all white with foam, indicating the worft
fpot, the noife of which was like thunder, the air refounding
with the echo of the cataracts. After viewing and carefully
examining this place, and fearching along the river bank for
the dead bodies, another very light fhallop having proceeded
meanwhile on the other bank alfo, we returned without finding anything.

CHAPTER III.

CHAMPLAIN'S EXPLANATION OF THE ACCOMPANYING MAP.

LE GRAND SAULT ST. LOUIS.

A. Small place that I had cleared up. *B.* Small pond. *C.* Small iflet, where
I had a ftone wall made. *D.* Small brook, where the barques are kept. *E.*
Meadows where the favages ftay when they come to this region. *F.* Mountains
feen in the interior. *G.* Small pond. *H.* Mont Royal. *I.* Small brook. *L.* The
fall. *M.* Place on the north fide, where the favages transfer their canoes by
land. *N.* Spot where one of our men and a favage were drowned. *O.* Small
rocky iflet. *P.* Another iflet where birds make their nefts. *Q.* Heron ifland.
R. Another ifland in the fall. *S.* Small iflet. *T.* Small round iflet. *V.* Another
iflet half covered with water. *X.* Another iflet, where there are many river birds.
Y. Meadows. *Z.* Small river. 2. Very large and fine iflands. 3. Places which
are bare when the water is low, where there are great eddies, as at the main fall.
4. Meadows covered with water. 5. Very fhallow places. 6. Another little iflet.
7. Small rocks. 8. Ifland St. Hélène. 9. Small ifland without trees. 8. Marfhes
connecting with the great fall.

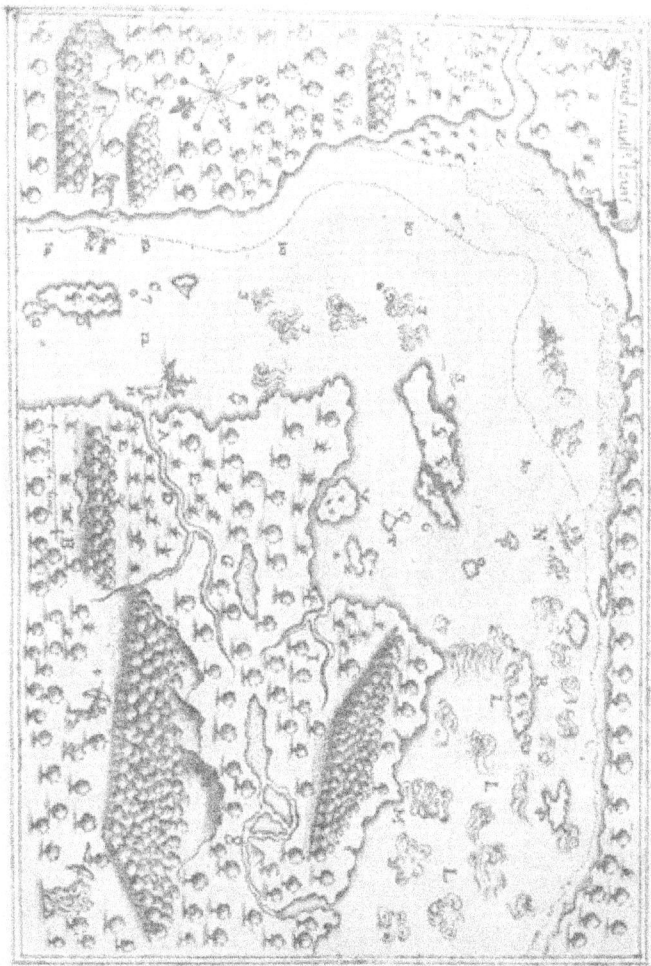

CHAPTER III.

Two Hundred Savages return the Frenchman who had been entrusted to them, and receive the Savage who had come back from France. — Various Interviews on both Sides.

N the thirteenth day **of the** month[16] two hundred Charioquois[17] favages, together **with** the captains Ochateguin, Iroquet, and Tregouaroti, brother of our favage, brought back **my** fervant.[18] We were greatly pleafed to fee them. I **went to** meet them in a canoe with our favage. As they were approaching flowly and in order, our men prepared to falute them with a difcharge of arquebufes, mufkets, and fmall pieces. When they were near at hand, they all fet to fhouting together, and one of the chiefs **gave** orders that they fhould make their harangue, in which they greatly praifed us, commending us as truthful, inafmuch as I had kept the promife to meet them at this fall. After they had made three more fhouts, there was a difcharge of mufketry twice from thirteen barques or patches that were there. This alarmed them fo, that they begged me to affure them that there fhould be no more firing, faying that the greater part of them had never feen Chriftians, nor heard thunderings of that fort, and that

they

[16] June 13th.

[17] *Charioquois.* In the iffue of 1632, p. 397, Champlain has *Sauvages Hurons.* It is probable that Charioquois was only a chief of the Hurons.

[18] This was the young man that had been fent to pafs the winter with the Indians, in exchange for the favage which had accompanied Champlain to France. *Vide antea,* Vol. II. p. 246.

they were afraid of its **harming** them, but that they were greatly pleafed **to fee our** favage in health, whom they fuppofed was dead, **as had** been reported by fome Algonquins, **who had heard fo from** the Montagnais. The favage commended the treatment I had fhown him in France, and the remarkable objects he had feen, at which all wondered, and went away quietly to their cabins, expecting that on the next day I would fhow them the place where I wifhed to have them dwell. I faw alfo my fervant, who was dreffed in the coftume of the favages, who commended the treatment he had received from them. He informed me of all he had feen and learned during the winter, from the favages.

The next day I fhowed them a fpot for their cabins, in regard to which the elders and principal ones confulted very privately. After their long confultation they fent for me alone and my fervant, who had learned their language very well. They told him they defired a clofe alliance with me, and were forry to fee here all thefe fhallops, and that our favage had told them he did not know them at all nor their intentions, and that it was clear that they were attracted only by their defire of gain and their avarice, and that when their affiftance was needed they would refufe it, and would not act as I did in offering to go with my companions to their country and affift them, of all of which I had given them proofs in the paft. They praifed me for the treatment I had fhown our favage, which was that of a brother, and had put them under fuch obligations of good will to me, that they faid they would endeavor to comply with anything I might defire from them, but that they feared
that

that the other boats would do them fome harm. I affured
them that they would not, and that we were all under **one**
king, whom our favage had feen, and belonged to the fame
nation, though matters of bufinefs were confined to individuals, and that they had no occafion to fear, but might
feel as much fecurity as if they were in their own country.
After confiderable converfation, they made me a prefent of
a hundred caftors. I gave them in exchange other kinds
of merchandife. They told me there were more **than** four
hundred favages of their country who had purpofed to come,
but had been prevented by the following reprefentations of
an Iroquois prifoner, who had belonged to me, but had efcaped to his own country. He had reported, they faid, that
I had given him his liberty and fome merchandife, and that
I purpofed to go to the fall with fix hundred Iroquois to
meet the Algonquins and kill them all, adding that the fear
aroufed by this intelligence had alone prevented them from
coming. I replied that the prifoner in queftion had efcaped
without my leave, that our favage knew very well how he
went away, and that there was no thought of abandoning
their alliance, as they had heard, fince I had engaged in war
with them, and fent my fervant to their country to fofter
their friendfhip, which was ftill farther confirmed by my
keeping my promife to them in fo faithful a manner.

They replied that, fo far as they were concerned, they
had never thought of this; that they were well aware that
all this talk was far from the truth, and that if they had
believed the contrary they would not have come, but that
the others were afraid, never having feen a Frenchman
except my fervant. They told me alfo that three hundred
Algonquins

Algonquins would come in five or six days, if we would wait for them, to unite with themselves in war againft the Iroquois; that, however, they would return without doing fo unlefs I **went.** I **talked a** great deal with them about the **fource of the** great river and their country, and they gave me detailed information about their rivers, falls, lakes and lands, as alfo about the tribes living there, and what is to be found in the region. Four of them affured me that they had feen a fea at a great diftance from their country, but that it was difficult to go there, not only on account of the wars, but of the intervening wildernefs. They told me alfo that the winter before fome favages had come from the direction of Florida, beyond the country of the Iroquois, who lived near our ocean, and were in alliance with thefe favages. In a word, they made me a very exact ftatement, indicating by drawings all the places where they had been, and taking pleafure in talking to me about them; and for my part I did not tire of liftening to them, as they confirmed points in regard to which I had been before in doubt. After all this converfation was concluded, I told them that we would trade for the few articles they had, which was done the next day. Each one of the barques carried away its portion; we on our fide had all the hardfhip and venture; the others, who had not troubled themfelves about any explorations, had the booty, the only thing that urges them to activity, in which they employ no capital and venture nothing.

The next day, after bartering what little they had, they made a barricade about their dwelling, partly in the direction of the wood, and partly in that of our pataches; and this they faid they did for their fecurity, in order to avoid the
surprifes

furprifes of their enemies, which we took for the **truth.** **On** the coming night, they called our favage, who was fleeping on my patache, and my fervant, who went to them. After a great deal of converfation, about midnight they had me called alfo. Entering their cabins, I found them all feated in council. They had me fit down near them, faying that when they met for the purpofe of confidering a matter, it was their cuftom to do fo at night, that they might not be diverted by anything from attention to **the** fub-**ject** in hand; that at night one thought only of liftening, while during the day the thoughts were diftracted by other objects.

But in my opinion, confiding in me, they defired to tell me privately their purpofe. Befides, they were afraid of the other pataches, as they fubfequently gave me to underftand. For they told me that they were uneafy at feeing fo many Frenchmen, who were not efpecially united to one another, and that they had defired to fee me alone; that fome of them had been beaten; that they were as kindly difpofed towards me as towards their own children, confiding fo much in me that they would do whatever I told them to do, but that they greatly miftrufted the others; that if I returned I might take as many of their people as I wifhed, if it were under the guidance of a chief; and that they fent for me to affure me anew of their friendfhip, which would never be broken, and to exprefs the hope that I might never be ill difpofed towards them; and being aware that I had deter-mined to vifit their country, they faid they would fhow it to me at the rifk of their lives, giving me the affiftance of a large number of men, who could go everywhere; and that

in

in future we fhould expect fuch treatment from them as they had received from us.

Straightway they brought fifty caftors and four ftrings of beads, which they value as we do gold chains, faying that I fhould fhare thefe with my brother, referring to Pont Gravé, we being prefent together; that thefe prefents were fent by other captains, who had never feen me; that they defired to continue friends to me; that if any of the French wifhed to go with them, they fhould be greatly pleafed to have them do fo; and that they defired more than ever to eftablifh a firm friendfhip. After much converfation with them, I propofed that inafmuch as they were defirous to have me vifit their country, I would petition His Majefty to affift us to the extent of forty or fifty men, equipped with what was neceffary for the journey, and that I would embark with them on condition that they would furnifh us the neceffary provifions for the journey, and that I would **take prefents** for the chiefs of the country through which we fhould pafs, when we would return to our fettlement to fpend the winter; that moreover, if I found their country favorable and fertile, we would make many fettlements there, by which means we fhould have frequent intercourfe with each other, living happily in the future in the fear of God, whom we would make known to them. They were well pleafed with this propofition, and begged me to fhake hands upon it, faying that they on their part would do all that was poffible for its fulfilment; that, in regard to provifions, we fhould be as well fupplied as they themfelves, affuring me again that they would fhow me what I defired to fee. Thereupon, I took leave of them at daybreak, thanking them for

their

their willingnefs to carry out my wifhes, and entreating
them to continue to entertain the fame feelings.

On the next day, the 17th, they faid that they were going
caftor-hunting, and that they would all return. On the following morning they finifhed bartering what little they had,
when they embarked in their canoes, afking us not to take
any fteps towards taking down their dwellings, which we
promifed them. Then they feparated from each other, pre-
tending to go a hunting in different directions. They left
our favage with me that we might have lefs diftruft in **them.**
But they had appointed themfelves a rendezvous above the
fall, where they knew well enough that we could not go
with our barques. Meanwhile, we awaited them in accordance with what they had told us.

The next day there came two favages, one Iroquet, the
other the brother of our Savignon. They came to get the
latter, and afk me in behalf of all their companions to go
alone with my fervant to where they were encamped, as
they had fomething of importance to tell me, which they
were unwilling to communicate to any Frenchmen. I
promifed them that I would go.

The following day I gave fome trifles to Savignon, who
fet out much pleafed, giving me to underftand that he was
about to live a very irkfome life in comparifon with that
which he had led in France. He exprefled much regret at
feparation, but I was very glad to be relieved of the care
of him. The two captains told me that on the morning of
the next day they would fend for me, which they did. I
embarked, accompanied by my fervant, with thofe who came.
Having arrived at the fall, we went fome eight leagues into

the

the woods, where they were encamped on the fhore of a lake, where I had **been** before.[19] They were much pleafed at feeing me, and **began to** fhout after their cuftom. Our Indian **came out to** meet me, and afk me to go to the cabin **of his brother,** where he at once had fome meat and fifh **put on** the **fire** for my entertainment. While I was there, a banquet was held, to which all the leading Indians were invited. I was not forgotten, although I had already eaten fufficiently; but, in order not to violate the cuftom of the country, I attended. After banqueting, they went into the woods to hold their council, and meanwhile I amufed my-felf in looking at the country round about, which is very pleafant.

Some time after they called me, in order to communi-cate to me what they had refolved upon. I proceeded to them accordingly with my fervant. After I had feated myfelf by their fide, they faid they were very glad to fee me, and to find that I had not failed to keep my word in what I had promifed them; faying that they felt it an additional proof of my affection that I continued the alliance with them, and that before fetting out they defired to take leave of me, as it would have been a very great difappointment to them to go away without feeing me, thinking that I would in that cafe have been ill difpofed towards them. They faid alfo that what had led them to fay they were going a hunt-ing, and build the barricade, was not the fear of their ene-mies nor the defire of hunting, but their fear of all the other pataches accompanying me, inafmuch as they had heard it

faid

---

[19] This was doubtlefs on the Lake of Two Mountains.

said that on the night they sent for me they were all **to be** killed, and that I should not be able to protect them **from** the others who were much more numerous; so that in order to get away they made use of this ruse. But they said if there had been only our two pataches they would have stayed some days longer, and they begged that, when I returned with my companions, I would **not** bring any others. To this I replied that I did not bring these, but that they followed without my invitation; that in the future, however, I would come in another manner; at which explanation **they** were much pleased.

And now they began again to repeat what they had promised me in regard to the exploration of the country, while I promised, with the help of God, to fulfil what I had told them. They besought me again to give them a man, and I replied that if there was any one among us who was willing to go, I should be well pleased.

They told me there was a merchant, named Bouyer, com-**mander of** a patache, who had asked them to take a young man, which request, however, they had been unwilling to grant before ascertaining whether this was agreeable to me, as they did not know whether we were friends, since he had come in my company to trade with them; also that they were in no wise under any obligations to him, but that he had offered to make them large presents.

I replied that we were in no wise enemies, and that they had often seen us conversing with each other; but that in regard to traffic each did what he could, and that the above-named Bouyer was perhaps desirous of sending this young man as I had sent mine, hoping for some return

in

in the future, which I could alfo lay claim to from them; that, however, they muft judge towards whom they had the greateft obligations, and from whom they were to expect the **moft**.

They **faid there** was no comparifon between the obligations in the two cafes, not only in view of the help I had rendered them in their wars againft their enemies, but alfo of the offer of my perfonal affiftance in the future, in all of which they had found me faithful to the truth, adding that all depended on my pleafure. They faid moreover that what made them fpeak of the matter was the prefents he had offered them, and that, if this young man fhould go with them, it would not put them under fuch obligations to this Bouyer as they were under to me, and that it would have no influence upon the future, fince they only took him on account of the prefents from Bouyer.

I replied that it was indifferent to me whether they took him or not, and in fact that if they took him for a fmall confideration I fhould be difpleafed at it, but if in return for valuable prefents, I fhould be fatisfied, provided he ftayed with Iroquet; which they promifed me. Then there was made on both fides a final ftatement of our agreements. They had with them one who had three times been made prifoner by the Iroquois, but had been fuccefsful in efcaping. This one refolved to go, with nine others, to war, for the fake of revenge for the cruelties his enemies had caufed him to fuffer. All the captains begged me to diffuade him if poffible, fince he was very valiant, and they were afraid that, advancing boldly towards the enemy, and fupported by a fmall force only, he would never return. To fatisfy them I endeavored

to

to do fo, and urged all the reafons I could, which, however, availed little; for he, fhowing me a portion of his fingers cut off, alfo great cuts and burns on his body, as evidences of the manner they had tortured him, faid that it was impoffible for him to live without killing fome of his enemies and having vengeance, and that his heart told him he muft fet out as foon as poffible, as he did, firmly refolved to behave well.

After concluding with them, I afked them to take me back in our patache. To accomplifh this, they got ready eight canoes in order to pafs the fall, ftripping themfelves naked, and directing me to go only in my fhirt. For it often happens that fome are loft in paffing the fall. Confequently, they keep clofe to each other, fo as to render affiftance at once, if any canoe fhould happen to turn over. They faid to me, If yours fhould unfortunately overturn, not knowing how to fwim, you muft not think of abandoning it, and muft cling to the little pieces in the middle of it, for we can eafily refcue you. I am fure that even the moft felf-poffeffed perfons in the world, who have not feen this place nor paffed it in little boats fuch as they have, could not do fo without the greateft apprehenfion. But thefe people are fo fkilful in paffing falls, that it is an eafy matter for them. I paffed with them, which I had never before done, nor any other Chriftian, except my above-mentioned fervant. Then we reached our barques, where I lodged a large number of them, and had fome converfation with the before-mentioned Bouyer in view of the fear he entertained that I fhould prevent his fervant from going with the favages. They returned the next day with the young man, who proved expenfive to his mafter who had expected, in my opinion. to recover the loffes of his voyage, which were very confiderable, like thofe of many others.

One of **our young men** also determined to go with thefe favages, **who are** Charioquois, living at a diftance of fome **one hundred** and fifty leagues from the fall. He went with the brother of Savignon, one of the captains, who promifed me to fhow him all that could be feen. Bouyer's man went with the above-mentioned Iroquet, an Algonquin, who lives fome eighty leagues from the fall. Both went off well pleafed and contented.

After the departure of the favages, we awaited the three hundred others who, as had been told us, were to come, in accordance **with the** promife I had made them. Finding that they did **not** come, all the pataches determined to induce fome Algonquin favages, who had come from Tadouffac, to go **to** meet them, in view of a reward that would be given them on their return, which was to be at the lateft not over nine days from the time of their departure, fo that we might know whether to expect them or not, and be able to return to Tadouffac. This they agreed to, and a canoe left with this purpofe.

On the fifth of July a canoe arrived from the Algonquins, who were to come to the number of three hundred. From it we learned that the canoe which had fet out from us had arrived in their country, and that their companions, wearied by their journey, were refting, and that they would foon arrive, in fulfilment of the promife they had made ; that at moft they would not be more than eight days behindhand, but that there would be only twenty-four canoes, as one of their captains and many of their comrades had died of a fever that
had

had broken out among them. They alfo faid **that they had**
fent many to the war, which had hindered their progrefs.
We determined to wait for them.

But finding that this period had elapfed without their
arrival, Pont Gravé fet out from the fall on the eleventh of
the month, to arrange fome matters at Tadouffac, while I
ftayed to await the favages.

The fame day a patache arrived, bringing provifions for
the numerous barques of which our party confifted. For
our bread, wine, meat, and cider had given out fome days
before, obliging us to have recourfe to fifhing, the fine river
water, and fome radifhes which grow in great abundance in the
country ; otherwife we fhould have been obliged to return.
The fame day an Algonquin canoe arrived, affuring us that
on the next day the twenty-four canoes were to come, twelve
of them prepared for war.

On the twelfth the Algonquins arrived with fome little
merchandife. Before trafficking they made a prefent to a
Montagnais Indian, the fon of Anadabijou,[20] who had lately
died, in order to mitigate his grief at the death of his
father. Shortly after they refolved to make fome prefents
to all the captains of the pataches. They gave to each of
them ten caftors, faying they were very forry they had no
more, but that the war, to which moft of them were going,
was the reafon ; they begged, however, that what they offered
might be accepted in good part, faying that they were all
friends to us, and to me, who was feated near them, more
than to all the others, who were well difpofed towards
them

[20] Champlain's orthography is here *Aranadabigrau. Vide* Vol. I. pp. 236, 291.

them only on account of their caftors, and had not always affifted them like myfelf, whom they had never found double-tongued like the **reft.**

I replied that all thofe whom they faw gathered together were their friends; that, in cafe an opportunity fhould prefent itfelf, they would not fail to do their duty; that we were all friends; that they fhould continue to be well difpofed towards us; that we would make them prefents in return for thofe they gave us; and that they fhould trade in peace. This they did, and carried away what they could.

The next day they brought me privately forty caftors, affuring me of their friendfhip, and that they were very glad of the conclufion which I had reached with the favages who had gone away, and that we fhould make a fettlement at the fall, which I affured them we would do, making them a prefent **in** return.

After everything had been arranged, they determined to go and obtain the body of Outetoucos, who was drowned at the fall, as we have before mentioned. They went to the fpot where he had been buried, difinterred him and carried him to the ifland of St. Hélène, where they performed their ufual ceremony, which is to fing and dance over the grave with feftivities and banquets following. I afked them why they difinterred the body. They replied that if their enemies fhould find the grave they would do fo, and divide the body into feveral pieces, which they would then hang to trees in order to offend them. For this reafon they faid that they transferred it to a place off from the road, and in the moft fecret manner poffible.

On the 15th there arrived fourteen canoes, the chief
over

over which was named *Tecouehata.* Upon their arrival
all the other favages took up arms and performed fome
circular evolutions. After going around and dancing to
their fatisfaction, the others who were in their canoes
alfo began to dance, making various movements of the
body. After finifhing their finging, they went on fhore
with a fmall quantity of furs, and made prefents fimilar to
thofe of the others. Thefe were reciprocated by fome of
equal value. The next day they trafficked in what little
they had, and prefented me perfonally with thirty caftors,
for which I made them an acknowledgment. They begged
me to continue my good will to them, which I promifed to
do. They fpoke with me very efpecially refpecting certain
explorations towards the north, which might prove advan-
tageous; and faid, in reference to them, that if any one of
my company would like to go with them, they would fhow
him what would pleafe me, and would treat him as one of
their own children. I promifed to give them a young man,
at which they were much pleafed. When he took leave of
me to go with them, I gave him a detailed memorandum of
what he was to obferve while with them. After they had
bartered what little they had, they feparated into three parties; one for the war, another for the great fall, another for
a little river which flows into that of the great fall. Thus
they fet out on the 18th day of the month, on which day
we alfo departed.

The fame day we made the thirty leagues from this fall to
the Trois Rivières. On the 19th we arrived at Quebec, which
is alfo thirty leagues from the Trois Rivières. I induced the
moft of thofe in each boat to ftay at the fettlement, when I

had

had fome repairs made and fome rofe-bufhes fet out. I had alfo fome oak wood put on board to make trial of in France, not only **for marine** wainscoting, but alfo for windows. The **next day, the 20th of** July, I fet out. On the 23d I arrived **at Tadouffac,** whence I refolved to return to France, in accordance with the advice of Pont Gravé. After arranging matters relating to our fettlement, according to the directions which Sieur de Monts had given me, I embarked in the veffel of Captain Tibaut, of La Rochelle, on the 11th of Auguft. During our paffage we had an abundance of fifh, fuch as *orades*, mackerel, and *pilotes*, the latter fimilar to herrings, and found about certain planks covered with *pouffe-pieds*, a kind of fhell-fifh attaching itfelf thereto, and growing there gradually. Sometimes the number of thefe little fifh is fo great that it is furprifing to behold. We caught alfo fome porpoifes and other fpecies of fifh. The weather was favorable as far as Belle Ifle,[21] where we were overtaken by fogs, which continued three or four days. The weather then becoming fair, we fighted Alvert,[22] and arrived at La Rochelle on the 16th of September, 1611.

CHAPTER IV.

[21] Belle Ile. An ifland on the coaft of Brittany in France.
[22] *Alvert.* Arvert, a village near Marennes, which they fighted as they approached La Rochelle.

CHAPTER IV.

ARRIVAL AT LA ROCHELLE. — DISSOLUTION OF THE PARTNERSHIP BETWEEN SIEUR DE MONTS AND HIS ASSOCIATES, THE SIEURS COLIER AND LE GENDRE OF ROUEN. — JEALOUSY OF THE FRENCH IN REGARD TO THE NEW DISCOVERIES IN NEW FRANCE.

UPON my arrival at La Rochelle **I proceeded** to **vifit** Sieur de Monts, at Pons[22] in **Saintonge, to** inform him of all that had occurred **during** the expedition, and of the promife which the Ochateguins[24] and Algonquins had made me, on condition that **we** would affift them in their wars, as I had agreed. Sieur de Monts, after liftening to it all, determined to go to the Court to arrange the matter. I ftarted before him to go there alfo. But on the way I was unfortunately detained by the falling of a horfe upon me, which came near **killing me.** This fall detained me fome time; but as foon **as I had** fufficiently recovered from its effects I fet out again to complete my journey and meet Sieur de Monts at Fontainebleau, who, upon his return to Paris, had a conference with his affociates. The latter were unwilling to continue in the affociation, as there was no commiffion forbidding any others from going to the new difcoveries and trading with the inhabitants of the country. Sieur de Monts, feeing this, bargained with them for what remained at the fettlement at Quebec,

[22] De Monts was governor of Pons, a town fituated about ten miles fouth of Saintes, in the prefent department of Lower Charente.

[24] *Ochateguins. Vide* Vol. III. Quebec ed. p 169. They were Hurons, and Ochateguin is fuppofed to have been one of their chiefs. *Vide* Vol. II. note 321.

Quebec, in confideration of **a** fum of money which he gave them for their fhare. **He** fent alfo fome men to take care of the fettlement, **in the** expectation of obtaining a commiffion **from His** Majefty. But while he was engaged in the purfuit **of** this object fome important matters demanded his attention, fo that he was obliged to abandon it, and he left me the duty of taking the neceffary fteps for it. As I was about arranging the matter, the veffels arrived from New France with men from our fettlement, thofe whom I had fent into the interior with the favages. They brought me very important information, faying that more than two hundred favages had come, expecting to find me at the great fall of St. Louis, where I had appointed a rendezvous, with the intention of affifting them according to their requeft. But, finding that I had not kept my promife, they were greatly **difpleafed. Our** men, however, made fome apologies, which **were** accepted, and affured them that they would not fail to come the following year or never. The favages agreed to this on their part. But feveral others left the old trading-ftation of Tadouffac, and came to the fall with many fmall barques to fee if they could engage in traffic with thefe people, whom they affured that I was dead, although our men ftoutly declared the contrary. This fhows how jealoufy againft meritorious objects gets poffeffion of bad natures; and all they want is that men fhould expofe themfelves to a thoufand dangers, to difcover peoples and territories, that they themfelves may have the profit and others the hard-fhip. It is not reafonable that one fhould capture the lamb and another go off with the fleece. If they had been willing to participate in our difcoveries, ufe their means, and rifk

their

their perfons, they would have given evidence of their **honor** and noblenefs, but on the contrary they fhow clearly **that** they are impelled by pure malice that they may enjoy the fruit of our labors equally with ourfelves.

On this fubject, and to fhow how many perfons ftrive to pervert praifeworthy enterprifes, I will inftance again the people of St. Malo and others, who fay that the profit of thefe difcoveries belongs to them, **fince** Jacques Cartier, who firft vifited Canada and the iflands of New Foundland, **was from** their city; as if that city had contributed **to the** expenfes of thefe difcoveries of Jacques Cartier, who went there by the **order** and at the expenfe of King Francis I. in the years 1534 and 1535 to difcover thefe territories now called New France. If then Cartier made any difcovery at the expenfe of His Majefty, all his fubjects have the fame rights and liberties in them as the people of St. Malo, who cannot prevent others who make farther difcoveries at their **own** expenfe, as is fhown in the cafe of the difcoveries above **defcribed,** from profiting by them in peace. Hence they ought not to claim any rights if they themfelves make no contributions, and their reafons for doing fo are weak and foolifh.

To prove more conclufively that they who maintain this pofition do fo without any foundation, let us fuppofe that a Spaniard or other foreigner had difcovered lands and wealth at the expenfe of the King of France. Could the Spaniards or other foreigners claim thefe difcoveries and this wealth on the ground that the difcoverer was a Spaniard or foreigner? No! There would be no fenfe in doing fo, and they would always belong to France. Hence the people

of

of St. Malo cannot make thefe claims for the reafon which they give, that Cartier was a citizen of their city; and they can only take cognizance of the faſt that he was a citizen of theirs, and render him accordingly the praiſe which is his due.

Befides, Cartier in the voyage which he made never paſſed the great fall of St. Louis, and made no difcoveries north or fouth of the river St. Lawrence. His narratives give no evidence of it, in which he fpeaks only of the river Saguenay, the Trois Rivières and St. Croix, where he fpent the winter in a fort near our fettlement. Had he done fo, he would not have failed to mention it, any more than what he has mentioned, which fhows that he left all the upper part of the St. Lawrence, from Tadouſſac to the great fall, being a territory difficult to explore, and that he was unwilling to expofe himſelf or let his barques engage in the venture. So that what he did has borne no fruit until four years ago, when we made our fettlement at Quebec, after which I ventured to paſs the fall to help the favages in their wars, and fend among them men to make the acquaintance of the people, to learn their mode of living, and the charaſter and extent of their territory. After devoting ourfelves to labors which have been fo fuccefsful, is it not juſt that we fhould enjoy their fruits, His Majefty not having contributed anything to aid thofe who have aſſumed the refponfibilities of thefe undertakings up to the prefent time. I hope that God will at fome time incline him to do fo much for His fervice, his own glory and the welfare of his fubjeſts, as to bring many new peoples to the knowledge of our faith, that they may at laſt enjoy the heavenly kingdom.

NOTE.

Champlain here introduces an explanation of his two geographical maps of New France, and likewise his method of determining a meridian line. For convenience of use the maps are placed at the end of this work, and for the same reason these explanations are carried forward to p. 219, in immediate proximity to the maps which they explain. — EDITOR.

FOURTH VOYAGE

OF

SIEUR DE CHAMPLAIN,

CAPTAIN IN ORDINARY TO THE KING IN THE MARINE, AND
LIEUTENANT OF MONSEIGNEUR LE PRINCE DE
CONDÉ IN NEW FRANCE,

MADE IN THE YEAR 1613.

To the very high, powerful, and excellent Henri de Bourbon, Prince de Condé, First Prince of the Blood, First Peer of France, Governor and Lieutenant of His Majesty in Guienne.

Monseigneur,

The Honor that I have received from your Highness in being intrusted **with** *the discovery of New France has inspired in me the desire to pursue with still greater pains and zeal* **than ever** *the search for the North Sea. With this object in* **view I** *have made a voyage during the past year, 1613, relying* **on a man whom** *I had sent there and who assured me he had* **seen it,** *as you will perceive in this brief narrative, which I* **venture** *to present to your Excellence, and in* **which are particularly** *described all the toils and sufferings* **I have had in the** *undertaking. But although I regret* **having lost this year** *so far as the main object* **is** *concerned, yet my expectation, as in the first voyage, of obtaining more definite information respecting the subject from* **the savages,** *has been fulfilled. They have told me about* **various lakes** *and rivers in the north, in view of which, aside from their assurance that they know of this sea, it seems to me* **easy to** *conclude from the maps that it cannot be far from* **the** *farthest discoveries I have hitherto made. Awaiting* **a** *favorable time and opportunity to prosecute my plans, and praying God to preserve you, most happy Prince, in all prosperity, wherein consists my highest wish for your greatness. I remain in the quality of*

Your most humble and devoted servant,

SAMUEL DE CHAMPLAIN.

FOURTH VOYAGE

OF

SIEUR DE CHAMPLAIN,

CAPTAIN IN ORDINARY TO THE KING IN THE MARINE, AND
LIEUTENANT OF MONSEIGNEUR LE PRINCE DE
CONDÉ IN NEW FRANCE,

MADE IN THE YEAR 1613.

CHAPTER I.

WHAT LED ME TO SEEK FOR TERMS OF REGULATION. — A COMMISSION OB-
TAINED. — OPPOSITIONS TO THE SAME. — PUBLICATION AT LAST IN ALL
THE PORTS OF FRANCE.

THE defire which I have always had of making new difcoveries in New France, for the good, profit, and glory of the French name, and at the fame time to lead the poor natives to the knowledge of God, has led me to feek more and more for the greater facility of this undertaking, which can only be fecured by means of good regulations. For, fince individuals defire to gather the fruits of my labor without contributing to the expenfes and great outlays requifite for the fupport of the fettlements neceffary to a fuccefsful refult, this

this branch of trade is ruined by the greedine∫s of gain, which is ∫o great **that it** cau∫es merchants to ∫et out prematurely **in** order to arrive fir∫t in this country. By this means **they not** only become involved in the ice, but al∫o in their **own ruin, for,** from trading with **the ∫avages in** a ∫ecret **manner** and offering through rivalry with each other more merchandi∫e than is nece∫∫ary, they get the wor∫t of the bargain. Thus, while purpo∫ing to deceive their a∫∫ociates, they generally deceive them∫elves.

For this rea∫on, when I returned to France on the 10th of September, 1611, I ∫poke to Sieur de Monts about the matter, who approved of my ∫ugge∫tions; but his engagements not allowing him to pro∫ecute the matter at court, he left to me its whole management.

I then drew up a ∫tatement, which I pre∫ented to Pre∫ident Jeannin, who, being a man de∫irous of ∫eeing good undertakings pro∫per, commended my project, and encouraged me in its pro∫ecution.

But feeling a∫∫ured that tho∫e who love to fi∫h in troubled waters would be vexed at ∫uch regulations and ∫eek means to thwart them, it ∫eemed advi∫able to throw my∫elf into the hands of ∫ome power who∫e authority would prevail over their jealou∫y.

Now, knowing Mon∫eigneur le Comte de Soi∫∫ons [26] to be a prince devout and well di∫po∫ed to all holy undertakings, I addre∫∫ed my∫elf to him through Sieur de Beaulieu, councillor, and almoner in ordinary to the King, and urged upon

him

---

[26] For a brief notice of the Count de Soi∫∫ons, *vide* Vol. I. note 74 ; al∫o note by Laverdière, Quebec ed., p. 433.

him the importance of the matter, fetting forth the means of regulating it, the harm which diforder had heretofore produced, and the total ruin with which it was threatened, to the great difhonor of the French name, unlefs God fhould raife up fome one who would reanimate it and give promife of fecuring for it fome day the fuccefs which had hitherto been little anticipated. After he **had been** informed in regard to all the details of the fcheme and **feen the** map of **the** country which I had made, he promifed me, **under the** fanction of the King, to undertake the protectorate **of the** enterprife.

I immediately after prefented to His Majefty, and to the gentlemen of his Council, a petition accompanied by articles, to the end that it might pleafe him to iffue regulations for the undertaking, without which, as I have faid, it would fail. Accordingly his Majefty gave the direction and control to the before-mentioned Count, who then honored me with the **lieutenancy.**

Now as I was preparing to publifh the commiffion[26] of **the** King in all the ports and harbors of France, there occurred the ficknefs and greatly lamented death of the Count, which poftponed fomewhat the undertaking. But his Majefty at once committed the direction to Monfeigneur le Prince,[27] who proceeded in the execution of its duties, and, having in like manner honored me with the lieutenancy,[28] directed me to go on with the publication of the commiffion.

[26] This Commiffion, dated October 15, 1612, will be found in Champlain's iffue of 1632. *Vide* Quebec ed., p. 887.

[27] Henry de Bourbon. *Vide* Vol. I. p. 113, note 75.

[28] Champlain was appointed lieutenant of the Prince de Condé on the 22d day of November, 1612. *Vide* iffue of 1632, Quebec ed., p. 1072.

miſſion. But as ſoon as this was done, ſome marplots, who had no intereſt in the matter, importuned him to annul it, repreſenting to him **as** they claimed the intereſts of all the merchants of France, who had no cauſe for complaint, ſince **all were received** into the aſſociation and could not therefore **juſtly** be aggrieved. Accordingly, their evil intention being recognized, they were diſmiſſed, with permiſſion **only to** enter into the aſſociation.

During theſe altercations, it was impoſſible for me, as the time of my departure was very near at hand, to do anything for the habitation at Quebec, for repairing and enlarging which I deſired to take out ſome workmen. It was accordingly neceſſary to go out this year without any farther organization. The paſſports of Monſeigneur le Prince were made out for four veſſels, which were already in readineſs **for the** voyage, viz. three from Rouen and one from La **Rochelle, on** condition that each ſhould furniſh four men for my aſſiſtance, **not only** in my diſcoveries but in war, as I deſired to keep the promiſe which I had made to the Ochataiguins[20] in the year 1611, to aſſiſt them in their wars at the time of my next voyage.

As I was preparing to ſet out, I was informed that the Parliamentary Court of Rouen would not permit the publication of the commiſſion of the King, becauſe his Majeſty had reſerved to himſelf and his Council the ſole cognizance of the differences which might ariſe in this matter ; added to which was the fact that the merchants of St. Malo were alſo oppoſed to it. This greatly embarraſſed me, and obliged

me

---

[20] Ochateguins, or Hurons.

me to make three journeys to Rouen, with orders **of his** Majefty, in confideration of which the Court defifted from their inhibition, and the affumptions of the opponents were overruled. The commiffion was then publifhed in all the ports of Normandy.

CHAPTER II.

DEPARTURE FROM FRANCE.—WHAT TOOK PLACE UP TO OUR ARRIVAL AT THE FALLS.

SET out from Rouen on the 5th of March for Honfleur, accompanied by Sieur L'Ange, to affift me in my explorations, and in war if occafion fhould require.

On the next day, the 6th of the month, we embarked in the veffel of Sieur de Pont Gravé, immediately fetting fail, with a favorable wind.

On the 10th of April we fighted the Grand Bank, where **we feveral** times tried for fifh, but without fuccefs.

On the 15th we had a violent gale, accompanied by rain and hail, which was followed by another, lafting forty-eight hours, and fo violent as to caufe the lofs of feveral veffels on the ifland of Cape Breton.

On the 21ft we fighted the ifland and Cap de Raye.[30] On the 29th the Montagnais favages, perceiving us from All Devils' Point,[31] threw themfelves into their canoes and came

to

[30] The *ifland* refers to New Foundland. Cap de Raye, ftill known as Cape Ray, was on the fouthweftern angle of New Foundland.

[31] Now called Point aux Vaches. It was fometimes called All-Devils' Point. *Vide* note 136, Vol. I, p. 235.

to meet us, being fo thin and hideous-looking that I did not
recognize them. **At** once they began crying for bread, faying that **they were** dying of hunger. This led us to conclude **that** the winter had not been fevere, and confequently
the hunting poor, which matter we have alluded to in previous voyages.

Having arrived on board of our veffel they examined **the**
faces of all, and as I was not to be feen anywhere they afked
where Monfieur de Champlain was, and were anfwered that
I had remained in France. But this they would not think
of believing, and an old man among them came to me in a
corner where I was walking, not defiring to be recognized
as yet, and taking me by the ear, for he fufpected who it
was, faw the fcar of the arrow wound, which I received at
the defeat of the Iroquois. At this he cried out, and all the
others after him, with great demonftrations of joy, faying,
Your people are awaiting you at the harbor of Tadouffac.

The fame day **we** arrived at Tadouffac, and although we
had fet out laft, neverthelefs arrived firft, Sieur Boyer of
Rouen arriving with the fame tide. From this it is evident
that to fet out before the feafon is fimply rufhing into the
ice. When we had anchored, our friends came out to us,
and, after informing us how everything was at the habitation, began to drefs three *outardes*[81] and two hares, which

they

---

[81] *Outardes.* Sometimes written *hou-
tardes,* and *Oltardes.* The name outarde or buftard, the *otis* of ornithologifts,
a land bird of Europe, was applied to a
fpecies of goofe in Canada at a very early
period.

The outarde is mentioned by Cartier
in 1535, and the name may have been
originally applied by the fifhermen and
fur-traders at a much earlier period,
doubtlefs on account of fome fancied
refemblance which they faw to the
leffer buftard or outarde, which was
about the fize of the Englifh pheafant.
Vide Pennant's Britifh Zoology, Vol. I.
p. 379. Cartier, Champlain, Lefcarbot,

they had brought, throwing the entrails overboard, after which the poor favages rufhed, and, like famifhed beafts, devoured

Baron La Hontan, Potherie, and Charlevoix mention the outarde in catalogues of water-fowl in which *oye*, the goofe, is likewife mentioned. They very clearly diftinguifh it from the clafs which they commonly confidered *oyes*, or geefe. Cartier, for inftance, fays, Il y a auffi grand nombre d'oyfeaulx, fcauoir grues, ognes, *oultardes, oyes fauuages, blanches, & grifes*. Others fpeak of *outardes et oyes*. They do not generally defcribe it with particularity. Champlain, however, in defcribing the turkey, *cocq d'inde*, on the coaft of New England, fays, auffi gros qu'vne outarde, qui eft vne efpece d'oye. Father Pierre Biard writes, *et au mefme temps les outardes arriuent du midy, qui font groffes comnes au double des noftres*. From thefe ftatements it is obvious that the outarde was a fpecies of goofe, but was fo fmall that it could well be defcribed as a large duck. In New France there were at leaft four fpecies of the goofe, which might have come under the obfervation of the early navigators and explorers. We give them in the order of their fize, as defcribed in Coues' Key to North American Birds.

1. Canada Goofe, *Branta Canadenfis*, SCOPOLI, 36 inches.

2. Snow Goofe, *Anfer hyperboreus*, LINNÆUS, 30 inches.

3. Am. White-fronted Goofe, *Anfer albifrons*, LINNÆUS, 27 inches.

4. Brant Goofe, *Branta bernicla*, SCOPOLI, 24 inches.

Recurring to the ftatement of Cartier above cited, it will be obferved that he mentions, befides the outarde, wild geefe white and gray. The firft and largeft of the four fpecies above mentioned, the Canada goofe, *Branta Canadenfis*, is gray, and the two next, the Snow goofe

and White-fronted, would be claffified as white. This difpofes of three of the four mentioned. The outarde of Cartier would therefore be the fourth fpecies in the lift, viz. the Brant goofe, *Branta bernicla*. This is the fmalleft fpecies found on our northern coaft, and might naturally be defcribed, as ftated by Father Biard, as a large duck. It **is** obvious that the good Father could not have defcribed the Canada goofe, **the** largeft of the four fpecies, as a large duck, and the white geefe have never been fuppofed to be referred to under the name of outarde. The Brant goofe, to which all the evidence which we have been able to find in the Canadian authorities feems to point as the outarde of early times, is common in our markets in its feafon, but our market-men, unaccuftomed to make fcientific diftinctions, are puzzled to decide whether it fhould be claffed as a goofe or a duck. It is not improbable that the early voyagers to our northern latitudes, unable to decide to which of thefe claffes this water-fowl properly belonged, and feeing in it a fancied refemblance to the leffer outarde, with which they were familiar, gave it for fake of the diftinction, but neverthelefs inappropriately, the name of outarde. The reader is referred to the following authorities.

Vide Brief Récit par Jacques Cartier, 1545, D'Avezac ed., p. 33; *Champlain*, Quebec ed., p. 220; *Jéfuite Relations*, 1616, p. 10; *Le Grand Voyage du Pays des Hurons*, par Sagard. Paris, 1632, p. 301; *Dictionaire de la Langue Huronne*, par Sagard. Paris, 1632, *oyfeaux; Letters to the Dutchefs of Lefdiguieres*, by Fr. Xa. de Charlevoix, London, 1763, p. 88; *Le Jeune, Relations des Jéfuites*, 1633, p. 4, 1636, p. 47; *Hiftoire de l'Amérique*

devoured them without drawing. They alfo fcraped off
with their nails the fat with which our veffel had been
coated, eating it gluttonoufly as if they had found fome
great **delicacy.**

The next day two veffels arrived from St. Malo, which
had fet out before the oppofitions had been fettled and the
commiffion been publifhed in Normandy. I proceeded on
board, accompanied by L'Ange. The Sieurs de la Moinerie
and la Tremblaye were in command, to whom I read the
commiffion of the King, and the prohibition againft violating
it on penalties attached to the fame. They replied that they
were fubjects and faithful fervants of His Majefty, and that
they would obey his commands; and I then had attached to
a poft in the port the arms and commiffion of His Majefty,
that no ground for ignorance might be claimed.

On the 2d of May, feeing two fhallops equipped to go
to the Falls, I embarked with the before-mentioned L'Ange
in one of them. We had very bad weather, fo that the
mafts of our fhallop were broken, and had it not been for
the preferving hand of God we fhould have been loft, as was
before our eyes a fhallop from St. Malo, which was going
to the Ifle d'Orleans, thofe on board of which however
being faved.

On the 7th we arrived at Quebec, where we found in good
condition thofe who had wintered there, they not having
been fick; they told us that the winter had not been fevere,
and that the river had not frozen. The trees alfo were
beginning to put forth leaves and the fields to be decked
with flowers.

On

l'Amérique Septentrionale, par de la 172, 212, 308; *Lefcarbot, Hiftoire de la
Potherie*, Paris, 1722, Vol. I. pp. 20, *Nouvelle France*, pp. 369, 582, 611.

On the 13th we fet out from Quebec for the Falls of St. Louis, where we arrived on the 21ft, finding there one of our barques which had fet out after us from Tadouffac, and which had traded fome with a fmall troop of Algonquins, who came from the war with the Iroquois, and had with them two prifoners. Thofe in the barque gave them to underftand that I had come with a number of men to affift **them** in their wars, according to the promife I had made **them in** previous years; alfo that I defired to **go** to their country and enter into an alliance with all their friends, at which they were greatly pleafed. And, inafmuch as they were defirous of returning to their country to affure their friends of their victory, fee their wives, and put to death their prifoners in a feftive *tabagie*, they left us pledges of their return, which they promifed fhould be before the middle of the firft moon, according to their reckoning, their fhields made of wood and elk leather, and a part of their bows and arrows. I regretted very much that I was not prepared to go with them to their country.

Three days after, three canoes arrived with Algonquins, who had come from the interior, with fome articles of merchandife which they bartered. They told me that the bad treatment which the favages had received the year before had difcouraged them from coming any more, and that they did not believe that I would ever return to their country on account of the wrong impreffions which thofe jealous of me had given them refpecting me; wherefore twelve hundred men had gone to the war, having no more hope from the French, who, they did not believe, would return again to their country.

This

This intelligence greatly disheartened the merchants, as they had made a great purchase of merchandise, with the expectation that **the** savages would come, as they had been accustomed to. This led me to resolve, as I engaged in my **explorations, to** pass through their country, in order to encourage those who had stayed back, with an assurance of the good treatment they would receive, and of the large amount of good merchandise at the Fall, and also of the desire I had to assist them in their war. For carrying out this purpose I requested three canoes and three savages to guide us, but after much difficulty obtained only two and one savage, and this by means of some presents made them.

CHAPTER III.

DEPARTURE TO DISCOVER THE NORTH SEA, ON THE GROUND OF THE RE-
PORT MADE ME IN REGARD TO IT. DESCRIPTION OF SEVERAL RIVERS,
LAKES AND ISLANDS; THE FALLS OF THE CHAUDIÈRE AND OTHER FALLS.

OW, as I had only two canoes, I could take with me but four men, among whom was one named Nicholas de Vignau, the most impudent liar that has been seen for a long time, as the sequel of this narrative will show. He had formerly spent the winter with the savages, and I had sent him on explorations the preceding years. He reported to me, on his return to Paris in 1612, that he had seen the North Sea; that the river of the Algonquins came from a lake which emptied into it; and that in seventeen days one could go from the Falls of St. Louis to this sea and back again; that he had seen the wreck and *débris* of an English ship that had been wrecked.

on

on board of which were eighty men, who had efcaped **to**
the fhore, and whom the favages killed becaufe the Englifh endeavored to take from them by force their Indian corn
and other neceffaries of life; and that he had feen the fcalps
which thefe favages had flayed off, according to their cuf-
tom, which they would fhow me, and that they would likewife give me a young Englifh boy whom they had kept for
me. This intelligence had greatly pleafed me, for I thought
that I had almoft found that for which I had for a long time
been fearching. Accordingly I enjoined upon him to tell **me**
the truth, in order that I might inform the King, and warned
him that if he gave utterance to a lie he was putting the
rope about his neck, affuring him on the other hand that,
if his narrative were true, he could be certain of being well
rewarded. He again affured me, with ftronger oaths than
ever; and in order to play his *rôle* better he gave me a
defcription of the country, which he faid he had made as
well as he was able. Accordingly the confidence which I
faw in him, his entire franknefs as it feemed, the defcription
which he had prepared, the wreck and *débris* of the fhip,
and the things above mentioned, had an appearance of probability, in connection with the voyage of the Englifh to
Labrador in 1612, where they found a ftrait, in which they
failed as far as the 63d degree of latitude and the 290th of
longitude, wintering at the 53d degree and lofing some veffels, as their report proves.[28] Thefe circumftances inducing
me

---

[28] *Vide* Vol. II. p. 171, note 297, for
an account of Henry Hudfon, to whom
this ftatement refers. De Vignau had
undoubtedly heard rumors concerning
Hudfon's expedition to the bay that
bears his name in the years 1610-11,
out of which he fabricated the fine ftory
of his pretended difcovery. Longitude
at that time was reckoned from the
ifland of Ferro, one of the Canaries.
Proceeding

me to believe that what he faid was true. I made a report of
the fame to the Chancellor,[34] which I fhowed to Marfhal
de Briffac,[35] Prefident Jeannin,[36] and other Seigneurs of the
Court, **who** told me that I ought to vifit the place in perfon.
For this reafon I requefted Sieur Georges, a merchant of La
Rochelle, to give him a paffage in his fhip, which he willingly did, and during the voyage he queftioned him as to
his object in making it; and, fince it was not of any profit
to him, he afked if he expected any pay, to which the young
man anfwered that he did not, that he did not expect anything from any one but the King, and that he undertook
the voyage only to fhow me the North Sea, which he had
feen. He made an affidavit of this at La Rochelle before
two notaries.

Now as I took leave on Whitfuntide,[37] of all the principal
men to whofe prayers I commended myfelf, and alfo to thofe
of all others, I faid to him in their prefence that if what he had
previoufly

Proceeding from weft to eaft, the 290°
would pafs through Hudfon's Bay, as
may be feen by confulting any early
French map. *Vide* Bellin's *Carte du
Globe Terreftre*, 1764.

[34] Nicholas Brulart de Sillery, who
was born at Sillery, in France, in 1544,
and died in the fame place in 1624. He
rendered fignal fervice to Henry IV.
Among other public acts he negotiated
the peace of Vervins between France
and Spain in 1598. He was appointed
grand chancellor of France in 1607.
Henry IV. faid of him, Avec mon chan-
clier qui ne fait pas le latin et mon con-
netable (Henri de Montmorency), qui
ne fait ni lire ni écrire, je puis venir à
bout des affaires les plus difficiles.

[35] For fome account of Marfhal de
Briffac, *vide* Vol. i. p. 17, note 16.

[36] *Vide* Vol. i. p. 112, note 73. Prefident Jeannin was a moft fuitable perfon to confult on this fubject, as he was
deeply interefted in the difcovery of
a northweft paffage to India. When
minifter at the Hague he addreffed a
letter bearing date January 21ft, 1609,
to Henry IV. of France, containing an
account of his indirect negotiations with
Henry Hudfon, for a voyage to difcover
a fhorter paffage to India. A copy of
this interefting letter, both in French
and Englifh, may be found in *Henry
Hudfon the Navigator*, by G. M. Afher,
L.L.D., Hakluyt Society, London, 1860,
p. 243.

[37] The feftival of Whitfunday occurred on the 26th May. *Laverdière
in loco.*

previoufly faid was not true he muſt not give me the trouble
to undertake the journey, which involved many dangers.
Again he affirmed all that he had faid, on peril of his life.

Accordingly, our canoes being laden with fome proviſions,
our arms, and a few articles of merchandiſe for making preſents to the favages, I fet out on Monday the 27th of May
from Iſle St. Hélène with four Frenchmen and one favage,
a parting falute being given me with fome rounds from
fmall pieces. This day we went only to the Falls **of** St.
Louis, a league up the river, the bad weather not allowing
us to go any farther.

On the 29th we paſſed the Falls,[38] partly by land, partly by
water, it being neceſſary for us to carry our canoes, clothes,
victuals, and arms on our ſhoulders, no fmall matter for perfons not accuſtomed to it. After going two leagues beyond
the Falls, we entered a lake,[39] about twelve leagues in circuit,
into which three rivers empty; one coming from the weſt,
from the direction of the Ochateguins, diſtant from one
hundred and fifty to two hundred leagues from the great
Falls;[40] another from the fouth and the country of the
Iroquois, a like diſtance off;[41] and the other from the north
and the country of the Algonquins and Nebicerini, alſo
about the fame diſtance.[42] This river on the north, according

[38] The Falls of St. Louis.

[39] Lake St. Louis.

[40] Champlain is here ſpeaking of the
river St. Lawrence, which flows into
Lake St. Louis ſlightly fouth of weſt.

[41] Rivière de Loup, now known as
the Chateauguay.

[42] The River Ottawa or a branch of
it flows into Lake St. Louis from the
north, although its courſe is rather from
the weſt. It was often called the River
of the Algonquins. It approaches com-
paratively near to Lake Nipiſſing, the
home of the Nipiſſirini. The fources
of the Ottawa are northeaſt of Lake
Nipiſſing, a diſtance of from one to three
hundred miles. The diſtances here given
by Champlain are only general eſtimates
gathered from the Indians, and are
neceſſarily inaccurate.

ing to the report of the favages, comes from a fource more remote, and paffes by tribes unknown to them and about three hundred leagues diftant.

This lake is filled with fine large iflands, containing only pafturage land, where there is fine hunting, deer and fowl being plenty. Fifh are abundant. The country bordering the lake is covered with extenfive forefts. We proceeded to pafs the night at the entrance to this lake, making barricades againft the Iroquois, who roam in thefe regions in order to furprife their enemies; and I am fure that if they were to find us they would give us as good a welcome as them, for which reafon we kept a good watch all night. On the next day I took the altitude of the place, and found it in latitude 45° 18′. About three o'clock in the afternoon we entered the river which comes from the north, and, paffing a fmall fall[43] by land fo as to favor our canoes, we proceeded to a little ifland, where we fpent the remainder of **the** night.

On the laft day of May we paffed another lake,[44] feven or eight leagues long and three broad, containing feveral iflands. The neighboring country is very level, except in fome places, where there are pine-covered hills. We paffed a fall called by the inhabitants of the country Quenechouan,[45] which is filled with ftones and rocks, and where the water runs with great velocity. We had to get into the water and drag our canoes along the fhore with a rope. Half a

league

[43] Rapide de Bruffi, by which the river flows from the Lake of Two Mountains into Lake St. Louis.

[44] *Lac de Soiffons*, now called Lake of Two Mountains. *Vide* Vol. I. p. 294.

[45] This is the firft of a feries of falls now known as the Long Fall.

league from there we paffed another little fall by rowing,
which makes one fweat. Great fkill is required in paffing
thefe falls, in order to avoid the eddies and furf, in which
they abound; but the favages do this with the greateft poffible dexterity, winding about and going by the eafiest places,
which they recognize at a glance.

On Saturday, the 1ft of June, we paffed two other falls;
the firft half a league long, the fecond **a** league, in which
we had much difficulty; for the rapidity of the **current is fo**
great that it makes a frightful noife, and produces, as it defcends from ftage to ftage, fo white a foam everywhere that
the water cannot be feen at all. This fall is ftrewn with
rocks, and contains fome iflands here and there covered with
pines and white cedars. This was the place where we had
a hard time; for, not being able to carry our canoes by land
on account of the denfity of the wood, we had to drag them
in the water with ropes, and in drawing mine I came near
lofing my life, as it croffed into one of the eddies, and if I
had not had the good fortune to fall between two rocks the
canoe would have dragged me in, inafmuch as I was unable
to undo quickly enough the rope which was wound around
my hand, and which hurt me feverely and came near cutting
it off. In this danger I cried to God and began to pull my
canoe, which was returned to me by the refluent water, fuch
as occurs in thefe falls. Having thus efcaped I thanked
God, begging Him to preferve us. Later our favage came to
help me, but I was out of danger. It is not ftrange that
I was defirous of preferving my canoe, for if it had been loft
it would have been neceffary to remain, or wait until fome
favages came that way, a poor hope for thofe who have

nothing

nothing to dine on, and who are not accuſtomed to ſuch hardſhip. As for our Frenchmen, they did not have any better luck, and ſeveral times came near loſing their lives; **but** the Divine Goodneſs preſerved us all. During the **remainder** of the day we reſted, having done enough.

The next day we fell in with fifteen canoes of ſavages called *Quenongebin,*[46] in a river, after we had paſſed a ſmall lake, four leagues long and two broad. They had been informed of my coming by thoſe who had paſſed the Falls of St. Louis, on their way from the war with the Iroquois. I was very glad to meet them, as were they alſo to meet me, but they were aſtoniſhed to ſee me in this country with ſo few companions, and with only one ſavage. Accordingly, after ſaluting each other after the manner of the country, I deſired them not to go any farther until I had informed them of my plan. To this they aſſented, and we encamped on an iſland.

The next day I explained to them that I was on my way to their country to viſit them, and fulfil the promiſe I had previouſly made them, and that if they had determined to go to the war it would be very agreeable to me, inaſmuch as I had brought ſome companions with this view, at which they were greatly pleaſed; and having told them that I wiſhed to go farther in order to notify the other tribes, they wanted to deter me, ſaying that the way was bad, and that we had ſeen nothing up to this point. Wherefore I aſked them to give me one of their number to take charge of our
ſecond

---

[46] *Quenongebin.* Lavernière makes this the ſame as the Kinounchepirini of Vimont. It was an Algonquin na-   tion ſituated ſouth of Allumette Iſland. *Vide Jeſuite Relations,* Quebec ed., 1640, p. 34.

fecond canoe, and alfo to ferve us as guide, fince **our** con-
ductors were not acquainted any farther. This they did
willingly, and in return I made them a prefent and gave
them one of our Frenchmen, the leaft indifpenfable, whom I
fent back to the Falls with a leaf of my note-book, on which
for want of paper I made a report of myfelf.

Thus we parted, and continuing our courfe up the river
we found another one, very fair and broad, which comes
from a nation called *Ouefcharini*,[47] who live north of it, **a**
diftance of four days' journey from the mouth. This **river**
is very pleafant in confequence of the fine iflands it contains, and the fair and open woods with which its fhores are
bordered. The land is very good for tillage.

On the fourth day we paffed near another river coming
from the north, where tribes called *Algonquins* live. This
river falls into the great river St. Lawrence, three leagues
below the Falls of St. Louis, forming a large ifland of nearly
forty leagues.[48] This river is not broad, but filled with a
countlefs number of falls, very hard to pafs. Sometimes
thefe

[47] *Ouefcharini.* Thefe people, called Ouaouechkairini by Viment, appear to have dwelt on the ftream now known as the *Rivière de Petite Nation*, rifing in a fyftem of lakes, among which are Lake Simon, Whitefifh Lake, Long Lake, and Lake Des Ifles. *Vide Jéfuite Relations*, 1640, p. 34. The tribe here mentioned was fubfequently called the Little Nation of the Algonquins: hence the name of the river. *Laverdière.*

[48] This paffage is exceedingly obfcure. Laverdière fuppofes that part of a fen-tence was left out by the printer. If fo it is remarkable that Champlain did not correct it in his edition of 1632. Laver-dière thinks the river here fpoken of is the Gatineau, and that the favages fol-lowing up this ftream went by a port-age to the St. Maurice, and paffing down reached the St. Lawrence *thirty* leagues, and not *three*, below the Falls of Saint Louis. The three rivers thus named inclofe or form an ifland of about the extent defcribed in the text. This ex-planation is plaufible. The paffage amended would read, "This river *ex-tends near another which* falls into the great river St. Lawrence thirty leagues below the falls of St. Louis." We know of no other way in which the paffage can be rationally explained.

thefe tribes go by way of this river in order to avoid encounters with their enemies, knowing that they will not try
to find them in places fo difficult of accefs.

Where this river has its debouchure is another coming from
the fouth,[49] at the mouth of which is a marvellous fall. For
it defcends a height of twenty or twenty-five fathoms[50] with
fuch impetuofity that it makes an arch nearly four hundred
paces broad. The favages take pleafure in paffing under it,
not wetting themfelves, except from the fpray that is thrown
off. There is an ifland in the middle of the river which, like
all the country round about, is covered with pines and white
cedars. When the favages defire to enter the river they
afcend the mountain, carrying their canoes, and go half a
league by land. The neighboring country is filled with all
forts of game, fo that the favages often make a ftop here.
The Iroquois alfo go there fometimes and furprife them
while making the paffage.

We paffed a fall[51] a league from there, which is half a
league broad, and has a defcent of fix or feven fathoms.
There are many little iflands, which are, however, nothing
more than rough and dangerous rocks covered with a poor
fort

[49] Rideao, at the mouth of which is Green Ifland, referred to in the text below.

[50] The fall in the Rideau is thirty-four feet, according to the Edinburgh Gazetteer of the World. The eftimate of Champlain is fo far out of the way that it feems not unlikely that feet were intended inftead of fathoms. *Vide* Vol. I. pp. 301, 302.

[51] The Chaudière Falls, juft above the prefent city of Ottawa, the greateft height of which is about forty feet. "Arrayed in every imaginable variety of form, in vaft dark maffes, in graceful cafcades, or in tumbling fpray, they have been well defcribed as a hundred rivers ftruggling for a paffage. Not the leaft interefting feature they prefent is the Loft Chaudière, where a large body of water is quietly fucked down, and difappears under ground." *Vide Canada* by W. H. Smith. Vol. I. p. 120. Alfo Vol. I. p. 120 of this work.

fort of brufhwood. The water falls in one place with **fuch**
force upon a rock that it has hollowed out in courfe of **time**
a large and deep bafin, in which the water has a circular
motion and forms large eddies in the middle, fo that the
favages call it *Aflicon*, which fignifies boiler. This cataraét
produces fuch a noife in this bafin that it is heard for more
than **two** leagues. The favages when paffing here obferve
a ceremony which we fhall fpeak of in its place. **We** had
much trouble in afcending by rowing againft a ftrong cur-
rent, in order to reach the foot of the fall. Here the favages
took their canoes, my Frenchmen and myfelf our arms, provifions, and other neceffaries, and we paffed over the rough
rocks for the diftance of about a quarter of a league, the
extent of the fall. Then we embarked, being obliged afterwards to land a fecond time and go about three hundred
paces through copfe-wood, after which we got into the water
in order to get our canoes over the fharp rocks, the trouble
attending which may be imagined. I took the altitude of
this place, which I found to be in latitude 45° 38'.[82]

In the afternoon we entered a lake,[83] five leagues long and
two wide, in which there are very fine iflands covered with
vines, nut-trees, and other excellent kinds **of trees.** Ten or
twelve leagues above we paffed fome iflands covered with
pines. The land is fandy, and there is found here a root
which dyes a crimfon color, with which the favages paint
their faces, as alfo little gewgaws after their manner. There
is alfo a mountain range along this river, and the furround-
ing country feems to be very unpromifing. The reft of the
day we paffed on a very pleafant ifland. The

[82] The latitude of the Chaudière Falls is about 45° 27'.   [83] Chaudière Lake, which was only an expanfion of the River Ottawa.

The next day we proceeded on our courſe to a great fall, nearly three leagues broad, in which the water falls a height of ten or twelve fathoms in a ſlope, making a marvellous noiſe.[54] **It is filled** with a vaſt number of iſlands, **covered with pines and** cedars. In order to paſs it we were obliged to give up our maize or Indian corn, and ſome few other proviſions we had, together with our leaſt neceſſary clothes, retaining only our arms and lines, to afford us means of ſupport from hunting and fiſhing as place and luck might permit. Thus lightened we paſſed, ſometimes rowing, ſometimes carrying our canoes and arms by land, the fall, which is a league and a half long,[55] and in which our ſavages, who are indefatigable in this work and accuſtomed to endure ſuch hardſhips, aided us greatly.

Continuing our courſe, we paſſed two other falls, one by land, the other with oar and poles ſtanding up. Then we entered a lake,[56] ſix or ſeven leagues long, into which flows a river coming from the ſouth,[57] on which at a diſtance of five days' journey from the other river[58] live a people called *Matou-oüeſcarini*.[59] The lands about the before-mentioned lake are ſandy and covered with pines, which have been almoſt entirely burned down by the ſavages. There are ſome

---

[54] Rapide des Chats.

[55] This probably refers to that part of the fall which was more difficult to paſs.

[56] Lake des Chats. The name *des chats* appears to have been given to this Lake, the Rapids, and the *Nation des chats,* on account of the great number of the *loup cervier,* or wild cats, *chats ſauvages,* found in this region. Cf. *Le Grande Voyage du Pays des Hurons,* par Sagard, Paris, 1632, p. 307.

[57] Madawaſka River, an affluent of the Ottawa, uniting with it at Fitz Roy.

[58] Probably an alluſion to the River St. Lawrence.

[59] This is the ſame tribe alluded to by Vimont under the name, *Mataouch-karini,* as dwelling ſouth of Allumette Iſland. *Vide Relations des Jéſuites,* 1640, Quebec ed., p. 34.

fome iflands, in one of which we refted ourfelves. Here **we** faw a number of fine red cypreffes,[60] the firft I had feen in this country, out of which I made a crofs, which I planted at one end of the ifland, on an elevated and confpicuous fpot, with the arms of France, as I had done in other places where we had flopped. I called this ifland *Sainte Croix.*

On the 6th we fet out from this ifland of St. Croix, where **the** river is a league and a half broad, and having made eight or ten leagues we paffed a fmall fall by oar, and a number of iflands of various fizes. Here our favages **left the** facks containing their provifions and their lefs neceffary articles, in order to be lighter for going overland and avoiding feveral falls which it was neceffary to pafs. There was a great difpute between our favages and our impoftor, who affirmed that there was no danger by way of the falls, and that we ought to go that way. Our favages faid to him, You are tired of living, and to me, that I ought not to believe him, and that he did not tell the truth. Accordingly, **having** feveral times obferved that he had no knowledge of **the places,** I followed the advice of the favages, which was fortunate for me, for he fought for dangers in order to ruin me or to difguft me with the undertaking, as he has fince confeffed, a ftatement of which will be given hereafter. We croffed accordingly towards the weft the river, which extended northward. I took the altitude of this place and found it in latitude 46° 40′.[61] We had much difficulty in

going

[60] *Cyprès,* Red Cedar or Savin, *Juniperus Virginiana. Vide* Vol. II. note 168.

[61] They were now, perhaps, two miles below Portage du Fort, at the point on the Ottawa neareft to the fyftem of lakes through which they were to pafs, and where, as ftated in the text, the Ottawa, making an angle, begins to flow directly from the north. The latitude, as here given,

going this diftance overland. I, for my part, was loaded only with three arquebufes, as many oars, my cloak, and fome fmall articles. **I** cheered on our men, who were fomewhat **more heavily** loaded, but more troubled by the mofquitoes **than by their** loads. Thus after paffing four fmall ponds and **having** gone a diftance of two and a half leagues, we were **fo** wearied that it was impoffible to go farther, not having eaten for twenty-four hours anything but a little broiled fifh without feafoning, for we had left our provifions behind, as I mentioned before. Accordingly we refted on the border of a pond, which was very pleafant, and made a fire to drive away the mofquitoes, which annoyed us greatly, whofe perfiftency is fo marvellous that one cannot defcribe it. Here we caft our lines to catch fome fifh.

The next day we paffed this pond, which was perhaps a league long. Then we went by land three leagues through a country worfe than we had yet feen, fince the winds had blown down the pines on top of each other. This was no flight inconvenience, as it was neceffary to go now over, now under, thefe trees. In this way we reached a lake, **fix** leagues long and two wide,[62] very abundant in fifh, **the** neighboring

given, is even more than ufually incorrect, being too high by more than a degree. The true latitude is about 45° 37'. *Vide Walker* and *Miles's Atlas of Dominion of Canada.* Note 62 will explain the caufe of this inexactnefs.

[62] Mufkrat Lake. On Champlain's map of 1612 will be feen laid down a fucceffion of lakes or ponds, together with the larger one, now known as Mufkrat Lake, on the borders of which are figured the dwellings of the favages referred to in the text. The pond which they paffed is the laft in the feries before reaching Mufkrat Lake. On the direct route between this pond and the lake, known as the Mufkrat Portage road, the courfe undoubtedly traverfed by Champlain, there was found in 1867, in the townfhip of Rofs, an aftrolabe, an inftrument ufed in taking latitudes, on which is the date, 1603. It is fuppofed to have been loft by Champlain on his prefent expedition. The reafons for this fuppofition have been ftated in feveral brochures recently iffued, one by Mr. O. H. Marfhall of Buffalo,

neighboring people doing their fifhing there. Near this lake is a fettlement of favages, who till the foil and gather har-
vefts

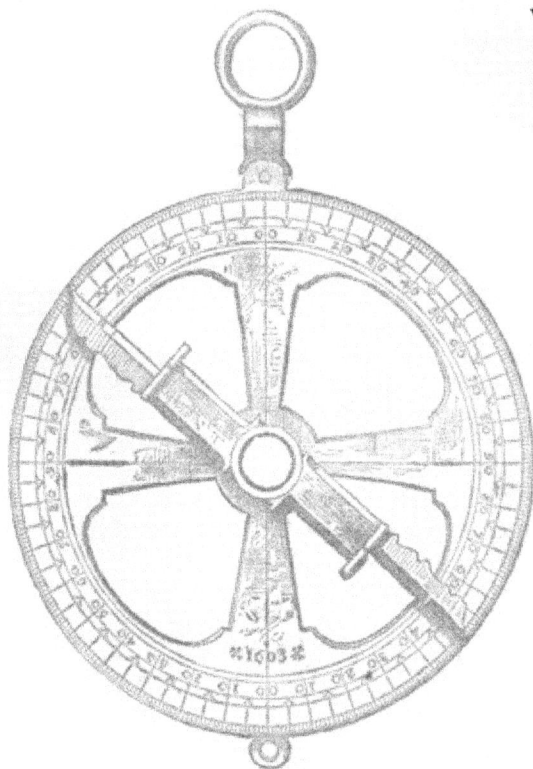

Buffalo, entitled *Difcovery of an Aftro-labe fuppofed to have been loft by Cham-plain in* 1613, New York, 1879; reprinted from the *Magazine of American Hif-tory*

9

vefts of maize. Their chief is named *Nibachis*, who came to
vifit us with his followers, aftonifhed that we could have
passed

tery for March of that year. Another,
*Champlain's Aftrolabe loft on the 7th
of June*, 1613, *and found in Auguft*,
1867, by A. J. Ruffell of Ottawa, Montreal, 1879. And a third entitled *The
Aftrolabe of Samuel Champlain and
Geoffrey Chaucer*, by Henry Scadding,
D. D., of Toronto, 1880. All of thefe writers agree in the opinion that the inftrument was probably loft by Champlain
on his expedition up the Ottawa in 1613.
For the argument *in extenfo* the reader
is referred to the brochures above cited.

Mr. Ruffell, who examined the aftrolabe thus found with great care and
had it photographed, defcribes it as a
circular plate having a diameter of five
inches and five eighths. " It is of plate
brafs, very dark with age, one eighth of
an inch thick above, increafing to fix
fixteenths of an inch below, to give it
fteadinefs when fufpended, which apparently was intended to be increafed
by hanging a weight on the little projecting ring at the bottom of it, in ufing
it on fhip-board. Its fufpending ring
is attached by a double hinge of the
nature of a univerfal joint. Its circle is
divided into fingle degrees, graduated
from its perpendicular of fufpenfion.
The double-bladed index, the pivot of
which paffes through the centre of the
aftrolabe, has flits and eyelets in the
projecting fights that are on it."

We give on the preceding page an engraving of this aftrolabe from a pho-
tograph, which prefents a fufficiently
accurate outline of the inftrument. The
plate was originally made to illuftrate
Mr. Marshall's article in the Magazine
of American Hiftory, and we are in-
debted to the courtefy of the proprietors
of the Magazine, Meffrs. A. S. Barnes
and Company of New York, for its ufe
for our prefent purpofe.

The aftrolabe, as an inftrument for
taking the altitude of the ftars or the
fun, had long been in ufe. Thomas
Blundevile, who wrote in 1622, fays he
had feen three kinds, and that the aftrolabe of Stofflerus had then been in ufe a
hundred years. It had been improved
by Gemma Frifius. Mr. Blagrave had
likewife improved upon the laft-men-
tioned, and his inftrument was at that
time in general ufe in England. The
aftrolabe continued to be employed in
Great Britain in taking altitudes for
more than a century fubfequent to this,
certainly till Hadley's Quadrant was invented, which was firft announced in
1731.

The aftrolabes which had the broad-
eft difks were more exact, as they were
projected on a larger fcale, but as they
were eafily jolted by the wind or the
movement of the fhip at fea, they could
with difficulty be employed. But Mr.
Blundevile informs us that " the Spaniards doe commonly make their aftrolabes narrow and weighty, which for the
moft part are not much above five inches
broad, and yet doe weigh at the leaft
foure pound, & to that end the lower
part is made a great deale thicker then
the upper part towards the ring or
handle." *Vide M. Blundevile his Ex-
ercifes*, London, 1622, pp. 595, 597.
This Spanish inftrument, it will be obferved, is very fimilar to that found on
the Old Portage road, and the latter may
have been of Spanish make.

In order to take the latitude in Champlain's day, at leaft three diftinct fteps
or proceffes were neceffary, and the
following directions might have been
given.

1. Let the aftrolabe be fufpended fo
that it fhall hang plumb. Direct the index
or diopter to the fun at noon, fo that the
fame

paffed the falls and bad roads in order to reach them. **After** offering us tobacco, according to their cuftom, he began to addrefs his companions, faying, that we muft have fallen from the clouds, for he knew not how we could have made the journey, and that they who lived in the country had much trouble in traverfing thefe bad ways: and he gave them to underftand that I accomplifhed all that I fet my mind **upon**; in fhort, that he believed refpecting **me all** that the other favages had told him. Aware **that we were hungry,** he gave us fome fifh, which we ate, and after our **meal I** explained **to** him, through Thomas, our interpreter, the pleafure I had in meeting them, that I had come to this country to affift them in their wars, and that I defired to go ftill farther to fee fome other chiefs for the fame object, at which they were glad and promifed me affiftance. They fhowed me their gardens and the fields, where they had maize. Their foil is fandy, for which reason they devote **themfelves** more to hunting than to tillage, unlike the Ochateguins.

fame ray of light may fhine through both holes in the two tablets or pinnules on the diopter, and the diopter will point to the degree of the fun's meridian altitude indicated on the outer rim of the aftrolabe.

II. Afcertain the exact degree of the fun's declination for that day, by a table calculated for that purpofe, which accompanies the aftrolabe.

III. Subtract the declination, fo found, if it be northerly, from the meridian altitude; or if the declination be foutherly, add the declination to the meridian altitude, and the refult, fubtracted from 90°, will give the latitude.

In thefe feveral proceffes of taking the latitude there are numerous poffi-

bilities of inexactnefs. It does not appear that any correction was made for refraction of light, or the preceffion of the equinoxes. But the moft important fource of inaccuracy was in the ufe of the aftrolabe whofe difk was fo fmall that its divifions could not be carried beyond degrees, and confequently minutes were arrived at by fheer eftimation, and ufually when the work was completed, the error was not lefs than one fourth or one half of a degree, and it was often much more.

This accounts fully for the inaccuracies of Champlain's latitudes from firft to laft throughout his entire explorations, as tefted by the very exact inftruments and tables now in ufe. No better method of

Ochateguins,[62] When they wish to make a piece of land arable, they burn down the trees, which is very easily done, as they are all pines, and filled with rosin. The trees having been burned, they dig up the ground a little, and plant their **maize** kernel by kernel,[63] like those in Florida. At the time I was there it was only four fingers high.

CHAPTER **IV.**

CONTINUATION. — ARRIVAL AT THE ABODE OF TESSOUAT, AND HIS FAVORABLE RECEPTION OF ME. — CHARACTER OF THEIR CEMETERIES. — THE SAVAGES PROMISE ME FOUR CANOES FOR CONTINUING MY JOURNEY; WHICH THEY HOWEVER SHORTLY AFTER REFUSE. — ADDRESS OF THE SAVAGES TO DISSUADE ME FROM MY UNDERTAKING, IN WHICH THEY REPRESENT ITS DIFFICULTIES — MY REPLY TO THESE OBJECTIONS. — TESSOUAT ACCUSES MY GUIDE OF LYING, AND OF NOT HAVING BEEN WHERE HE SAID HE HAD. — THE LATTER MAINTAINS HIS VERACITY. — I URGE THEM TO GIVE ME CANOES. — SEVERAL REFUSALS. — MY GUIDE CONVICTED OF FALSEHOOD, **AND HIS** CONFESSION.

IBACHIS had two canoes fitted out, **to con**duct me to another chief, named *Tessouat*,[64] who lived eight leagues from him, on the border of a great lake, through which flows the river which we had left, and which extends northward. Accordingly we crossed the lake in a west-northwesterly direction, **a** distance of nearly seven leagues. Landing

of determining the latitude existed at that day, and consequently the historian is warned not to rely upon the latitude alone as given by the early navigators and explorers in identifying the exact localities which they visited.

[62] Subsequently called Hurons.

[63] *Vide* Vol. I. p. 49; Vol. II. note 219.

[64] It seems not improbable, as suggested by Laverdière, that this was the same chief that Champlain met at Tadoussac in 1603, then called *Besouat*. *Vide* Vol. I. p. 242.

ing there, we went a league towards the northeaſt through
a very fine country, where are ſmall beaten paths, along
which one can go eaſily. Thus we arrived on the ſhore of
the lake,[66] where the dwelling of Teſſoüat was. He was
accompanied by a neighboring chieftain, and was greatly
amazed to ſee me, ſaying that he thought I was a dream, and
that he did not believe his eyes. Thence we croſſed on to an
iſland,[67] where their cabins are, which are poorly conſtructed
out of the bark of trees. The iſland is covered with oaks,
pines, and elms, and is not ſubject to inundations, like the
other iſlands in the lake.

This iſland is ſtrongly ſituated ; for at its two ends, and
where the river enters the lake, there are troubleſome falls,
the roughneſs of which makes the iſland difficult of acceſs.
They have accordingly taken up their abode here in order
to avoid the purſuit of their enemies. It is in latitude 47°,[68]
as alſo the lake, which is twenty leagues long,[69] and three or
four wide. It abounds in fiſh ; the hunting, however, is not
eſpecially good.

On viſiting the iſland, I obſerved their cemeteries, and
was

---

[66] They croſſed Muſkrat Lake, and
after a portage of a league, by general
eſtimation, they reached Lake Allumette.
This lake is only the expanded current
of the river Ottawa on the ſouthern ſide
of Allumette Iſland, which is formed by
the bifurcation of the Ottawa.

[67] Allumette Iſland, often called, in
the *Relations des Jéſuites*, ſimply the
Iſland. The ſavages in occupation were
in the habit of exacting tribute from the
Hurons and others, who paſſed along on
their war excurſions or their journeys
for trade with the French at Montreal.
They bartered their maize with other

tribes for ſkins with which they clothed
themſelves.

[68] The true latitude here is about
45° 47'. On the map of 1632 the latitude correſponds with the ſtatement in
the text.

[69] In his iſſue of 1632 Champlain cor-
rects his ſtatement as to the length of
Allumette Iſland, and ſays it is ten
leagues long, which is nearly correct.
Vide Quebec ed. p. 868. Of this iſland
Bouchette ſays that in length it is about
fifteen miles, and on an average four
miles wide. *Britiſh Dominions in North
America*, London, 1831, Vol. I. p. 187.

was ftruck with wonder as I faw fepulchres of a fhape like fhrines, made of pieces of wood fixed in the ground at a dif- tance of **about** three feet from each other, and interfecting **at the upper end.** On the interfections above they place a **large piece** of wood, and in front another upright piece, on which is carved roughly, as would be expected, the figure of the male or female interred. If it is a man, they add a fhield, a fword attached to a handle after their manner, a mace, and bow and arrows. If it is a chief, there is a plume on his head, and fome other *matachia* or embellifh- ment. If it is a child, they give it a bow and arrow; if a woman or girl, a boiler, an earthen veffel, a wooden fpoon, and an oar. The entire fepulchre is fix or feven feet long at moft, and four wide; others are fmaller. They are painted yellow and red, with various ornaments as neatly done as the carving. The deceafed is buried with his drefs of beaver or other fkins which he wore when living, and they lay by his fide all his poffeffions, as hatchets, knives, boilers, and awls, fo that thefe things may ferve him in the land whither he goes; for they believe in the immortality of the foul, as I have elfewhere obferved. Thefe carved fepulchres are only made for the warriors; for in refpect to others they add no more than in the cafe of women, who are confidered a ufelefs clafs, accordingly but little is added in their cafe.

Obferving the poor quality of the foil, I afked them what pleafure they took in cultivating land fo unpromifing, fince there was fome much better, which they left barren and wafte, as at the Falls of St. Louis. They anfwered that they were forced to do fo in order to dwell in fecurity, and that the roughnefs of the locality ferved them as a defence againft

their

their enemies. But they said that if I would make a settlement of French at the Falls of St. Louis, as I had promised,
they would leave their abode and go and live near us, confi-
dent that their enemies would do them no harm while we
were with them. I told them that we would this year collect wood and stone in order the coming year to build a fort
and cultivate the land; upon hearing which they raised a
great cry of applause. This conference having been finished, I asked all the chiefs and prominent men **among**
them to assemble the next day on the main land, **at the**
cabin of Tessoüat, who purposed to celebrate a *tabagie* in
my honor, adding that I would there tell them my plans.
This they promised, and sent word to their neighbors to
convene at the appointed place.

The next day all the guests came, each with his porringer
and wooden spoon. They seated themselves without order
or ceremony on the ground in the cabin of Tessoüat, who
distributed to them a kind of broth made of maize crushed
between two stones, together with meat and fish which was
cut into little pieces, the whole being boiled together with-
out salt. They also had meat roasted on coals, and fish
boiled apart, which he also distributed. In respect to myself,
as I did not wish any of their chowder, which they prepare
in a very dirty manner, I asked them for some fish and meat,
that I might prepare it in my own way, which they gave
me. For drink, we had fine clear water. Tessoüat, who
gave the *tabagie*, entertained us without eating himself,
according to their custom.

The *tabagie* being over, the young men, who are not
present at the harangues and councils, and who during the
tabagies

tabagies remain at the door of the cabins, withdrew, when all who remained began to fill their pipes, one and another offering **me one.** We then spent a full half-hour in this **occupation,** not a word being spoken, as is their custom.

After smoking amply during so long a period of silence, I explained to them, through my interpreter, that the object of my journey was none other than to assure them of my friendship, and of the desire I had to assist them in their wars, as I had before done; that I had been prevented from coming the preceding year, as I had promised them, because the king had employed me in other wars, but that now he had ordered me to visit them and to fulfil my promises, and that for this purpose I had a number of men at the Falls of St. Louis. I told them that I was making an excursion in their territory to observe the fertility of their soil, their lakes and rivers, and the sea which they had told me was in their country; and that I desired to see a tribe distant six days' journey from them, called the *Nebicerini*, in order to invite them also to the war, and accordingly I asked them to give me four canoes with eight savages to guide me to these lands. And since the Algonquins are not great friends of the Nebicerini,[19] they seemed to listen to me with greater attention.

After I had finished my discourse, they began again to smoke, and to confer among themselves in a very low voice respecting my propositions. Then Tessouat in behalf of all the

rest

---

[19] This tribe was subsequently known as the Nipissings, who dwelt on the borders of Lake Nipissing. They were distinguished for their sorceries, under the cover of which they appear to have practised impositions which naturally enough rendered other neighboring Algonquin tribes hostile to them.

reſt began and ſaid, that they had always regarded me **more** friendly towards them than any Frenchman they had **ſeen;** that the proofs they had of this in the paſt made their confidence eaſier for the future: moreover, that I had ſhown myſelf in reality their friend, by encountering ſo many riſks in coming to ſee them and invite them to the war, and that **all** theſe conſiderations obliged them **to feel as** kindly diſpoſed towards me as towards their own children. But they ſaid that I had the preceding year broken my promiſe, **that** two thouſand ſavages had gone to the Falls with the expectation of finding me ready to go to the war, and making me preſents, but that they had not found me and were greatly ſaddened, ſuppoſing that I was dead, as ſome perſons had told them. He ſaid alſo, that the French who were at the Falls did not want to help them in their wars, that they had been badly treated by certain ones, ſo that they had reſolved among themſelves not to go to the Falls again, and **that this** had cauſed them, as they did not expect to ſee **me again, to** go alone to the war, and that in fact twelve **hundred** of them had already gone. And ſince the greater part of their warriors were abſent, they begged me to poſtpone the expedition to the following year, ſaying that they would communicate the matter to all the people of their country. In regard to the four canoes, which I aſked for, they granted them to me, but with great reluctance, telling me that they were greatly diſpleaſed at the idea of ſuch an undertaking, in view of the hardſhips which I would endure; that the people there were ſorcerers, that they had cauſed the death of many of their own tribe by charms and poiſoning, on which account they were not their friends: moreover they

ſaid

said that, as it regards war, I was not to think of them, as they were little-hearted. With these and many other considerations they endeavored to deter me from my purpose.

But my sole desire on the other hand was to see this people, **and enter** into friendship with them, so that I might **visit the** North Sea. Accordingly, with a view to lessening the force of their objections, I said to them, that it was not far to the country in question; that the bad roads could not be worse than those I had already passed; that their witchcraft would have no power to harm me, as my God would preserve me from them; that I was also acquainted with their herbs, and would therefore beware of eating them; that I desired to make the two tribes mutual friends, and that I would to this end make presents to the other tribe, being assured that they would do something for me. In view of these reasons they granted me, as I have said, four canoes, at which I was very happy, forgetting all past hardships in the hope of seeing this sea, as I so much desired.

For the remainder of the day, I went out walking in their gardens, which were filled with squashes, beans, and our peas, which they were beginning to cultivate, when Thomas, my interpreter, who understands the language very well, came to inform me that the savages, after I had left them, had come to the conclusion, that if I were to undertake this journey I should die and they also, and that they could not furnish the promised canoes, as there was no one of them who would guide me, but that they wished me to postpone the journey until the next year, when they would conduct me with a good train to protect me from that people, in case they should attempt to harm me, as they are evil-disposed.

This

This intelligence greatly difturbed me, and I at once **went** to them and told them, that up to this day I had regarded them as men and truthful perfons, but that now they had fhown themfelves children and liars, and that if they would not fulfil their promifes, they would fail to fhow me their friendfhip ; that, however, if they felt it an inconvenience to give me four canoes they fhould only furnifh two and four favages.

They reprefented to me anew the difficulties attending the journey, the number of the falls, the bad character of **the** people, and that their reafon for refufing my requeft **was** their fear of lofing me.

I replied that I was forry to have them fhow themfelves to fo flight an extent my friends, and that I fhould never have believed it ; that I had a young man, fhowing them my impoftor, who had been in their country, and had not found all thefe difficulties which they reprefented, nor the **people** in queftion fo bad as they afferted. Then they be-**gan to** look at him, in particular Teffoüat the old captain, with whom he had paffed the winter, and calling him by name he faid to him in his language : Nicholas, is it true that you faid you were among the Nebicerini? It was long before he fpoke, when he faid to them in their language, which he fpoke to a certain extent: Yes, I was there. They immediately looked at him awry, and throwing them-felves upon him, as if they would eat him up or tear him in pieces, raifed loud cries, when Teffoüat faid to him : You are a downright liar, you know well that you flept at my fide every night with my children, where you arofe every morning ; if you were among the people mentioned, it was while

while sleeping. How could you have been so bold as to lead your chief to believe lies, and so wicked as to be willing to expose his life to so many dangers? You are a worth-**less** fellow, and he ought to put you to death more cruelly **than we do** our enemies. I am not astonished that he should so importune us on the assurance of your words.

I at once told him that he must reply to these people; and since he had been in the regions indicated, that he must give me proofs of it, and free me from the suspense in which he had placed me. But he remained silent and greatly terrified.

I immediately withdrew him from the savages, and conjured him to declare the truth of the matter, telling him that, if he had seen the sea in question, I would give him the reward which I had promised him, and that, if he had not seen it, he must tell me so without causing me farther trouble. Again he affirmed with oaths all he had before said, and that he would demonstrate to me the truth of it, if the savages would give us canoes.

Upon this, Thomas came and informed me, that the savages of the island had secretly sent a canoe to the Nebicerini, to notify them of my arrival. Thereupon, in order to profit by the opportunity, I went to the savages to tell them, that I had dreamed the past night that they purposed to send a canoe to the Nebicerini without notifying me of it, at which I was greatly surprised, since they knew that I was desirous of going there. Upon which they replied that I did them a great wrong in trusting a liar, who wanted to cause my death, more than so many brave chiefs, who were my friends and who held my life dear. I replied that

my

my man, meaning our impoſtor, had been in the aforeſaid
country with one of the relatives of Teſſoüat and had ſeen
the ſea, the wreck and ruins of an Engliſh veſſel, together
with eighty ſcalps which the ſavages had in their poſſeſſion,
and a young Engliſh boy whom they held as priſoner, and
whom they wiſhed to give me as a preſent.

When they heard me ſpeak of the ſea, veſſels, ſcalps of
the Engliſh, and the young priſoner, they **cried** out more
than before that he was a liar, and thus they afterwards
called him, as if it were the greateſt inſult they could have
done him, and they all united in ſaying that he ought to be
put to death, or elſe that he ſhould tell with whom he had
gone to the place indicated, and ſtate the lakes, rivers, and
roads, by which he had gone. To this he replied with aſſurance, that he had forgotten the name of the ſavage, although
he had ſtated to me his name more than twenty times, and
even on the previous day. In reſpect to the peculiarities of
the country, he had deſcribed them in a paper which he had
handed me. Then I brought forward the map and had
it explained to the ſavages, who queſtioned him in regard
to it. To this he made no reply, but rather manifeſted by
his ſullen ſilence his perverſe nature.

As my mind was wavering in uncertainty, I withdrew by
myſelf, and reflected upon the above-mentioned particulars
of the voyage of the Engliſh, and how the reports of our liar
were quite in conformity with it, alſo that there was little
probability of this young man's having invented all that, in
which caſe he would not have been willing to undertake the
journey, but that it was more probable that he had ſeen theſe
things, and that his ignorance did not permit him to reply to
the

the queftions of the favages. To the above is to be added the fact that, if the report of the Englifh be true, the North Sea cannot be farther diftant from this region than a hundred **leagues in** latitude, for I was in latitude 47° and in longitude **296°.**[71] **But** it may be that the difficulties attending the paffage of the falls, the roughnefs of the mountains covered with fnows, is the reafon why this people have no knowledge of the fea in queftion; indeed they have always faid that from the country of the Ochateguins it is a journey of thirty-five or forty days to the fea, which they fee in three places, a thing which they have again affured me of this year. But no one has fpoken to me of this fea on the north, except this liar, who had given me thereby great pleafure in view of the fhortnefs of the journey.

Now, when this canoe was ready, I had him fummoned into the prefence of his companions; and after laying before him all that had tranfpired, I told him that any further diffimulation was out of the queftion, and that he muft fay whether he had feen thefe things or not; that I was defirous of improving the opportunity that prefented itfelf; that I had forgotten the paft; but that, if I went farther, I would have him hung and ftrangled, which fhould be his fole reward. After meditating by himfelf, he fell on his knees and afked my pardon, declaring that all he had faid, both in France and

this

---

[71] The true latitude, as we have ftated, *antea*, note 61, is about 45° 37'; but on Champlain's map it correfponds with the ftatement in the text, and a hundred leagues north of where they then were, as his map is conftructed, would carry them to the place in the bay where Hudfon wintered, as ftated by Champlain, and as laid down on his fmall map included in this volume; but the longitude is incorrect, Allumette Ifland being two or three degrees eaft of longitude 296°, as laid down on Champlain's map of 1632.

this country, in refpect to the fea in queftion was falfe; that
he had never feen it, and that he had never gone farther
than the village of Teffoüat; that he had faid thefe things
in order to return to Canada. Overcome with wrath at
this, I had him removed, being unable to endure him any
longer in my prefence, and giving orders to Thomas to
inquire into the whole matter in detail; to whom he ftated,
that he did not believe that I would undertake the journey
on account of the dangers, thinking that **fome difficulty**
would prefent itfelf to prevent me from going on, as **in the**
cafe of thefe favages, who were not difpofed to lend me
canoes; and accordingly that the journey would be put off
until another year, when he being in France would be rewarded for his difcovery; but that, if I would leave him
in this country, he would go until he found the fea in queftion, even if he fhould die in the attempt. Thefe were his
words as reported to me by Thomas, but they did not give
me much fatisfaction, aftounded as I was at the effrontery
and malicioufnefs of this liar: and I cannot imagine how
he could have devifed this impofition, unlefs that he had
heard of the above-mentioned voyage of the Englifh, and in
the hope of fome reward, as he faid, had the temerity to
venture on it.

Shortly after I proceeded to notify the favages, to my
great regret, of the malignity of this liar, ftating that he had
confeffed the truth; at which they were delighted, reproach-
ing me with the little confidence I put in them, who were
chiefs and my friends, and who always fpoke the truth;
and who faid that this liar ought to be put to death, being
extremely malicious; and they added, Do you not fee that he
                                        meant

meant to caufe your death. Give him to us, and we promife you that he fhall not lie any more. And as they all went after him fhouting, their children alfo fhouting ftill more, I forbade them to do him any harm, directing them to keep **their** children alfo from doing fo, inafmuch as I wifhed to **take him to** the Falls to fhow him to the gentlemen there, to whom he was to bring fome falt water; and I faid that, when I arrived there, I would confult as to what fhould be done with him.

My journey having been in this manner terminated, and without any hope of feeing the fea in this direction, except in imagination, I felt a regret that I fhould not have employed my time better, and that I fhould have had to endure the difficulties and hardfhips, which however I was obliged patiently to fubmit to. If I had gone in another direction, according to the report of the favages, I fhould have made a beginning in a thing which muft be poftponed to another time. At prefent my only wifh being to return, I defired the favages to go to the Falls of St. Louis, where there were four veffels loaded with all kinds of merchandife, and where they would be well treated. This they communicated to all their neighbors. Before fetting out, I made a crofs of white cedar, which I planted in a prominent place on the border of the lake, with the arms of France, and I begged the favages to have the kindnefs to preferve it, as alfo thofe which they would find along the ways we had paffed; telling them that, if they broke them, misfortune would befall them, but that, if they preferved them, they would not be affaulted by their enemies. They promifed to do fo, and faid that I fhould find them when I came to vifit them again.

CHAPTER V

CHAPTER V.

OUR RETURN TO THE FALLS.— FALSE ALARM. — CEREMONY AT THE CHAU-
DIÈRE FALLS.— CONFESSION OF OUR LIAR BEFORE ALL THE CHIEF MEN.
—OUR RETURN TO FRANCE.

N the 10th of June I took leave of Teſſoüat, a good old captain, making him preſents, and promiſing him, if God preſerved me in health, to come the next year, prepared to **go to** war. He in turn promiſed to aſſemble a large number by that time, declaring that I ſhould ſee nothing but ſavages and arms which would pleaſe me ; he alſo directed his ſon to go with me for the ſake of company. Thus we ſet out with forty canoes, and paſſed by way[72] of the river we had left, which extends northward, and where we went on ſhore in order to croſs the lakes. On the way we met nine large canoes of the Oueſcharini, with forty ſtrong and power-ful men, who had come upon the news they had received ; we alſo met others, making all together ſixty canoes ; and we overtook twenty others, who had ſet out before us, each heavily laden with merchandiſe.

We paſſed ſix or ſeven falls between the iſland of the Algonquins[73] and the little fall,[74] where the country was very unpleaſant. I readily realized that, if we had gone in that

direction,

[72] By the Ottawa, which they had left a little below Portage du Fort, and not by the ſame way they had come, through the ſyſtem of ſmall lakes, of which Muſkrat lake is one. *Vide Carte de la Nouvelle France*, 1632, Vol. I. p. 304.

[73] Allumette Iſland.

[74] Near Gould's Landing, below or ſouth of Portage du Fort.— *Vide Cham-plain's Aſtrolabe*, by A. J. Ruſſell, Mont-real, 1879, p. 6.

11

direction, we fhould have had much more trouble, and would with difficulty have fucceeded in getting through: and it was not **without reafon** that the favages oppofed our liar, as **his only** object was to caufe my ruin.

Continuing our courfe ten or twelve leagues below the ifland of the Algonquins, we refted on a very pleafant ifland, which was covered with vines and nut-trees, and where we caught fome fine fifh. About midnight, there arrived two canoes, which had been fifhing farther off, and which reported that they had feen four canoes of their enemies. At once three canoes were defpatched to reconnoitre, but they returned without having feen anything. With this affurance all gave themfelves up to fleep, excepting the women, who refolved to fpend the night in their canoes, not feeling at eafe on land. An hour before daylight a favage, having dreamed that the enemy were attacking them, jumped up and ftarted on a run towards the water, in order to efcape, fhouting, They are killing me. Thofe belonging to his band all awoke dumfounded and, fuppofing that they were being purfued by their enemies, threw themfelves into the water, as did alfo one of our Frenchmen, who fuppofed that they were being overpowered. At this great noife, the reft of us, who were at a diftance, were at once awakened, and without making farther invefligation ran towards them: but as we faw them here and there in the water, we were greatly furprifed, not feeing them purfued by their enemies, nor in a ftate of defence, in cafe of neceffity, but only ready to facrifice themfelves. After I had inquired of our Frenchman about the caufe of this excitement, he told me that a favage had had a dream, and that he with

the

the reft had thrown themfelves into the water in order to
efcape, fuppofing that they were being attacked. Accordingly, the ftate of the cafe being afcertained, it all paffed off
in a laugh.

Continuing our way, we came to the Chaudière Falls,
where the favages went through with the cuftomary ceremony,
which is as follows. After carrying their canoes to the foot
of the Fall, they affemble in one fpot, where one of them
takes up a collection with a wooden plate, into which each
one puts a bit of tobacco. The collection having been **made,**
the plate is placed in the midft of the troupe, and all dance
about it, finging after their ftyle. Then one of the captains
makes an harangue, fetting forth that for a long time they
have been accuftomed to make this offering, by which means
they are infured protection againft their enemies, that otherwife misfortune would befall them, as they are convinced by
the evil fpirit; and they live on in this fuperftition, as in many
others, as we have faid in other places. This done, the
maker of the harangue takes the plate, and throws the to-
bacco into the midft of the caldron, whereupon they all
together raife a loud cry. Thefe poor people are fo fuperfti-
tious, that they would not believe it poffible for them to
make a profperous journey without obferving this ceremony
at this place, fince their enemies await them at this portage,
not venturing to go any farther on account of the difficulty
of the journey, whence they fay they furprife them there, as
they have fometimes done.

The next day we arrived at an ifland at the entrance to
a lake, and feven or eight leagues diftant from the great
Falls of St. Louis. Here while repofing at night we had
another

another alarm, the savages supposing that they had seen the
canoes of their enemies. This led them to make several
large **fires, which** I had them put out, representing to them
the harm which might result, namely, that instead of con-
cealing they would disclose themselves.

On the 17th of June, we arrived at the Falls of St. Louis,
where I found L'Ange, who had come to meet me in a
canoe to inform me, that Sieur de Maisonneuve of St. Malo
had brought a passport from the Prince for three vessels. In
order to arrange matters until I should see him, I assembled
all the savages and informed them that I did not wish them
to traffic in any merchandise until I had given them per-
mission, and that I would furnish them provisions as soon as
we should arrive; which they promised, saying that they were
my friends. Thus, continuing our course, we arrived at the
barques, where we were saluted by some discharges of cannon,
at which some of our savages were delighted, and others
greatly astonished, never having heard such music. After I
had landed, Maisonneuve came to me with the passport of
the Prince. As soon as I had seen it, I allowed him and his
men to enjoy the benefits of it like the rest of us; and I
sent word to the savages that they might trade on the next
day.

After seeing all the chief men and relating the particulars
of my journey and the malice of my liar, at which they were
greatly amazed, I begged them to assemble, in order that in
their presence, and that of the savages and his companions,
he might make declaration of his maliciousness; which
they gladly did. Being thus assembled, they summoned him,
and asked him, why he had not shown me the sea in the
north.

north, as he had promifed me at his departure. He replied that he had promifed fomething impoffible for him, fince he had never feen this fea, and that the defire of making the journey had led him to fay what he did, alfo that he did not fuppofe that I would undertake it; and he begged them to be pleafed to pardon him, as he alfo did me again, confeffing that he had greatly offended, and if I would leave him in the country, he would by his efforts repair the offence, and fee this fea, and bring back truftworthy intelligence· concerning it the following year; and in view of certain confiderations I pardoned him on this condition.

After relating to them in detail the good treatment I had received at the abodes of the favages, and how I had been occupied each day, I inquired what they had done during my abfence, and what had been the refult of their hunting excurfions, and they faid they had had fuch fuccefs that they generally brought home fix ftags. Once on St. Barnabas's day, Sieur du Parc, having gone hunting with two others, killed nine. Thefe ftags are not at all like ours, and there are different kinds of them, fome larger, others fmaller, which **refemble** clofely our deer.[75] They had alfo a very large number

[75] At that time there were to be found in Canada at leaft four fpecies of the Cervus Family.

1. The Moofe, *Cervus alces*, or *alces Americanus*, ufually called by the earlieft writers *orignal* or *orignac*. *Vide* Vol. I. pp. 264, 265. This is the largeft of all the deer family in this or in any other part of the world. The average weight has been placed at feven hundred pounds, while extraordinary fpecimens probably attain twice that weight.

2. The Wapiti, or American Elk, *Cervus elaphus*, or *Canadenfis*. This is the largeft of the known deer except the preceding. The average weight is probably lefs than fix hundred pounds.

3. The Woodland Caribou, *Cervus tarandus*. It is fmaller than the Wapiti. Its range is now moftly in the northern regions of the continent, but fpecimens are ftill found in Nova Scotia and New Brunfwick. The female is armed with antlers as well as the male, though they are fmaller.

4. The Common Deer, *Cervus Virginianus*

number of pigeons,[50] and alfo fifh, fuch as pike, carp, fturgeon, fhad, barbel, turtles, bafs, and other kinds unknown to us, on which they dined and fupped every day. They were alfo all **in better** condition than myfelf, who was reduced from **work** and the anxiety which I had experienced, not having eaten more than once a day, and that of fifh badly cooked and half broiled.

On the 22d of June, about 8 o'clock in the evening, the favages founded an alarm becaufe one of them had dreamed he had feen the Iroquois. In order to content them, all the men took their arms, and fome were fent to their cabins to reaffure them, and into the approaches to reconnoitre, fo that, finding it was a falfe alarm, they were fatisfied with the firing of fome two hundred mufket and arquebus fhots, after which arms were laid down, the ordinary guard only being left. This reaffured them greatly, and they were very glad to fee the French ready to help them.

After the favages had bartered their articles of merchandife and had refolved to return, I afked them to take with them two young men, to treat them in a friendly manner, fhow them the country, and bind themfelves to bring them back. But they ftrongly objected to this, reprefenting to me the trouble our liar had given me, and fearing that they would bring me falfe reports, as he had done. I replied that they were men of probity and truth, and that if they would not take them they were not my friends, whereupon they

refolved

glntanus. It has the wideft range of any of the deer family. It is ftill found in every degree of latitude from Mexico to Britifh Columbia. *Vide Antelope*

and Deer of America by John Dean Caton, LL. D., Bofton, 1877.

[51] *Palombes*. The paffenger, or wild pigeon, *Ectopiftes migratorius*.

refolved to do fo. As for our liar, none of the **favages** wanted him, notwithftanding my requeft to them **to take** him, and we left him to the mercy of God.

Finding that I had no further bufinefs in this country. I refolved to crofs in the firft veffel that fhould return to France. Sieur de Maifonneuve, having his ready, offered **me a** paffage, which I accepted; and **on the 27th** of June I fet out with Sieur L'Ange from the Falls, where we left the other veffels, which were awaiting the return of **the favages who** had gone to the war, and we arrived at Tadouffac on **the 6th of** July.

On the 8th **of** Auguft[77] we were enabled by favorable weather to fet fail. On the 18th we left Gafpé and Ifle Percée. On the 28th we were on the Grand Bank, where the green fifhery is carried on, and where we took as many fifh as we wanted.

On the 26th of Auguft we arrived at St. Malo, where I faw the merchants, to whom I reprefented the eafe of form**ing a good** affociation in the future, which they refolved to **do, as** thofe of Rouen and La Rochelle had done, after recognizing the neceffity of the regulations, without which it is impoffible to hope for any profit from thefe lands. May God by His grace caufe this undertaking to profper to His honor and glory, the converfion of thefe poor benighted ones, and to the welfare and honor of France.

---

[77] *Le 8 Aouft.* Laverdière fuggefts with much plaufibility that this fhould read "The 8th of July." Champlain could hardly have found it neceffary to remain at Tadouffac from the 6th of July to the 8th of Auguft for favorable weather to fail. If he had been detained by any other caufe, it would probably have been deemed of fufficient gravity to be fpecially mentioned.

VOYAGES

AND

DISCOVERIES IN NEW FRANCE,

From the year 1615 to the end of the year 1618.

BY

SIEUR DE CHAMPLAIN,

Captain in ordinary to the King in the Western Sea.

WHERE ARE DESCRIBED

THE MANNERS, CUSTOMS, DRESS, MODE OF WAR-
fare, hunting, dances, festivals, and method of burial of various
*savage peoples, with **many** remarkable experiences of the author*
*in this country, and **an account of the** beauty, fertility, and tem-*
perature of** the **same.

PARIS.

CLAUDE COLLET, in the Palace, at the gallery of the Prisoners.

———————

M. DC. XIX.

WITH AUTHORITY OF THE KING.

TO THE KING.

IRE,

This is a third volume containing a narrative
of what has tranſpired moſt worthy of note
during the voyages I have made to New France,
and its peruſal will, I think, afford your Majeſty greater
pleaſure than that of thoſe preceding, which only deſignate
the ports, harbors, ſituations, declinations, and other particulars, having more intereſt for navigators and ſailors than for
other perſons. In this narrative you will be able to obſerve
more eſpecially the manners and mode of life of theſe peoples
both in particular and in general, their wars, ammunition,
method of attack and of defence, their expeditions and retreats
in various circumſtances, matters about which thoſe intereſted
deſire information. You will perceive alſo that they are not
ſavage to ſuch an extent that they could not in courſe of time and
through aſſociation with others become civilized and cultivated.
You will likewiſe perceive how great hopes we cheriſh from
the long and arduous labors we have for the paſt fifteen years
ſuſtained, in order to plant in this country the ſtandard of
the

the crofs, and to teach the people the knowledge of God and the glory of His **holy** name, it being our defire to cultivate a feeling of charity **towards** His unfortunate creatures, which it is **our duty** to practife more patiently than any other thing, **especially as** there are many who have not entertained fuch purpofes, but have been influenced only by the defire of gain. Neverthelefs we may, I fuppofe, believe that thefe **are** the means which God makes ufe of for the greater promotion of the holy defire of others. As the fruits which the trees bear are from God, the Lord of the foil, who has planted, watered, and nourifhed them with an efpecial care, fo your Majefty can be called the legitimate lord of our labors, and the good refulting from them, not only becaufe the land belongs to you, but alfo becaufe you have protected us againft fo many perfons, whofe only object has been by troubling us to prevent the fuccefs of fo holy a determination, taking from us the power to trade freely in a part of your country, and ftriving to bring everything into confufion, which would be, in a word, preparing the way for the ruin of everything to the injury of your ftate. To this end your fubjects have employed every conceivable artifice and all poffible means which they thought could injure us. But all thefe efforts have been thwarted by your Majefty, affifted by your prudent council, who have given us the authority of your name, and fupported us by your decrees rendered in our favor. This is an occafion for increafing in us our long-cherifhed defire to fend communities and colonies there, to teach the people the knowledge of God, and inform them of the glory and triumphs of your Majefty, fo that together with the French language they may alfo acquire a French heart and fpirit, which, next to the fear of God,

will

will be infpired with nothing fo ardently as the defire to **ferve** you. Should our defign fucceed, the glory of it will be due, after God, to your Majefty, who will receive a thoufand bene-dictions from Heaven for fo many fouls faved by your inftru-mentality, and your name will be immortalized for carrying **the** glory **and** fceptre of the French as far to the Occident as **your** precurfors have extended it to the **Orient,** and over the **entire** habitable earth. This will augment **the** quality of MOST CHRISTIAN belonging to you above all the kings of the earth, and fhow that it is as much your due by merit as it is your own of right, it having been tranfmitted to you by your predeceffors, who acquired it by their virtues; for you have been pleafed, in addition to fo many other important affairs, to give your attention to this one, fo ferioufly neglected hith-erto, God's fpecial grace referving to your reign the publi-cation of His gofpel, and the knowledge of His holy name to fo many tribes who had never heard of it. And fome day **may** God's grace lead them, as it does us, to pray to Him **without** ceafing to extend your empire, and to vouchfafe a **thoufand** bleffings to your Majefty.

    SIRE,

        Your moft humble, moft faithful,
            and moft obedient fervant and fubject,

                     CHAMPLAIN.

PREFACE.

S in the various affairs of the world each thing ftrives for its perfection and the prefervation of its being, fo on the other hand does man intereft himfelf in the different concerns of others on fome account, either for the public good, or to acquire, apart from the common intereft, praife and reputation with fome profit. Wherefore many have purfued this courfe, but as for myfelf I have made choice of the moft unpleafant and difficult one of the perilous navigation of the feas; with the purpofe, however, not fo much of gaining wealth, as the honor and glory of God in behalf of my King and country, and contributing by my labors fomething ufeful to the public good. And I make declaration that I have not been tempted by any other ambition, as can be clearly perceived, not only by my conduct in the paft, but alfo by the narratives of my voyages, made by the command of His Majefty, in New France, contained in my firft and fecond books, as may be feen in the fame.

Should God blefs our purpofe, which aims only for His glory, and fhould any fruit refult from our difcoveries and arduous labors, I will return thanks to Him, and for Your Majefty's protection and affiftance will continue my prayers for the aggrandizement and prolongation of your reign.

EXTRACT FROM THE LICENSE OF THE KING.

BY favor and licenfe of the KING, permiffion is given to CLAUDE COLLET, merchant bookfeller in our city of Paris, to print, or have printed by fuch printer as fhall feem good to him, a book entitled, *Voyages and Difcoveries in New France, from the Year* 1615 *to the End of the Year* 1618. *By Sieur de Champlain,* **Captain** *in Ordinary to the King in the Weftern Sea.* All bookfellers and printers of our kingdom are forbidden to print or have printed, to fell wholefale or retail, faid book, except with the confent of faid Collet, for the time and term of fix years, beginning with the day when faid book is printed, on penalty of confif-cation of the copies, and a fine of four hundred *livres,* a half to go to us and a half to faid petitioner. It is our will, moreover, that this Licenfe fhould be placed at the com-mencement or end of faid book. This is our pleafure.

Given at Paris, the 18th day of May, 1619, and of our reign the tenth.

By the Council,

DE CESCAUD.

V O Y A G E

OF

SIEUR DE CHAMPLAIN TO NEW FRANCE,

MADE IN THE YEAR 1615.

HE ftrong love, which I have always cherifhed for the exploration of New France, has made me defirous of extending more and more my travels over the country, in order, by means of its numerous rivers, lakes, and ftreams, to obtain at laft a complete knowledge of it, and alfo to become acquainted with the inhabitants, with the view of bringing them to the knowledge of God. To this end I have toiled conftantly for the paft fourteen or fifteen years,[78] yet have been able to advance my defigns but little, becaufe I have not received the affiftance which was neceffary for the fuccefs of fuch an undertaking. Neverthelefs, without

[78] Champlain's firft voyage was made in 1603, and this journal was publifhed in 1619. It was therefore fully fifteen years fince his explorations began.

without losing courage, I have not ceased to push on, and visit various nations of the savages; and, by associating familiarly with them, I have concluded, as well from their conversation as from the knowledge already attained, that **there is no** better way than, **disregarding** all storms and difficulties, to have patience until **His Majesty shall** give **the** requisite attention to the matter, **and** meanwhile, not only to continue the exploration of the country, but also to learn the language, and form relations and friendships with the leading men of the villages and tribes, in order to lay the foundations of a permanent edifice, as well for the glory of God as for the renown of the French.

And His Majesty having transferred and intrusted the superintendence of this work to Monseigneur the Prince de Condé, the latter has, by his management, under the authority of His Majesty, sustained us against all sorts of jealousies and obstacles concerted by evil wishers. This has, as it were, animated me and redoubled my courage for the continuation of my labors in the exploration of New France, and with increased effort I have pushed forward in my undertaking into the mainland, and farther on than I had previously been, as will be hereafter indicated in the course of this narrative.

But it is appropriate to state first that, as I had observed in my previous journeys, there were in some places people permanently settled, who were fond of the cultivation of the soil, but who had neither faith nor law, and lived without God and religion, like brute beasts. In view of this, I felt convinced that I should be committing a grave offence if I did not take it upon myself to devise some

means

means of bringing them to the knowledge **of God.** To this end I exerted myfelf to find fome good friars, **with** zeal and affection for the glory of God, that I might perfuade them to fend fome one, or go themfelves, with me to thefe countries, and try to plant there the faith, or at **leaft** do what was poffible according to their calling, and **thus** to obferve and afcertain whether **any good** fruit could **be gathered** there. But fince **to attain this** object an expenditure would be required exceeding my **means,** and **for** other reafons, I deferred the matter for a while, in view of the difficulties there would be in obtaining what **was** neceffary **and** requifite in fuch an enterprife ; and fince, furthermore, no perfons offered to contribute to it. Neverthelefs, while continuing my fearch, and communicating my plan to various perfons, a man of diftinction chanced to prefent himfelf, whofe intimate acquaintance I enjoyed. This was Sieur Hoüel, Secretary of the King and Controller-**general** of the falt works at Brouage, a man of devoted **piety, and** of great zeal and love for the honor of God and the extenfion of His religion.[71] He gave me the following information, which afforded me great pleafure. He faid that he was acquainted with fome good religious Fathers, of the order of the Recollects, in whom he had confidence ; and that he enjoyed fuch intimacy and confidence with them that he could eafily induce them to confent to undertake the voyage ; and that, as to the neceffary means for fending out three or four friars, there would be no lack of

---

[71] *Vide Hiftoire du Canada,* par Sagard, Trofs ed., pp. 27, 28. The reader is likewife referred to the Memoir of Champlain, Vol. I. pp. 122–124.

of people of property who would give them what they
needed, offering for his part to affift them to the extent of
his ability; and, in fact, he wrote in relation to the fubject
to Father du Verger,[80] who welcomed with joy the under-
taking. and, in accordance with the recommendation of
Sieur Hoüel, communicated it to fome of his brethren, who,
burning with charity, offered themfelves freely for this holy
undertaking.

Now he was at that time in Saintonge, whence he fent
two men to Paris with a commiffion, though not with abfolute power, referving the reft to the Nuncio of our Holy
Father the Pope, who was at that time, in 1614, in France.[81]
He called upon thefe friars at their houfe in Paris, and was
greatly pleafed with their refolution. We then went all together to fee the Sieur Nuncio, in order to communicate to
him the commiffion, and entreat him to interpofe his autho-
ity in the matter. But he, on the contrary, told us that he
had no power whatever in fuch matters, and that it was to
their General that they were to addrefs themfelves. Notwithftanding this reply, the Recollects, in confideration of
the difficulty of the miffion, were unwilling to undertake
the journey on the authority of Father du Verger, fearing
that it might not be fufficient, and that the commiffion
might not be valid, on which account the matter was poftponed to the following year. Meanwhile they took counfel, and came to a determination, according to which all
arrangements were made for the undertaking, which was
to

80 Bernard du Verger, a man of ex-
alted virtue. — *Laverdière*.

81 Robert Ubaldini was nuncio at this
time. *Vide Laverdière in loco*.

to be carried out in the following fpring; awaiting which the two friars returned to their convent at Brouage.

I for my part improved the time in arranging my affairs in preparation for the voyage.

Some months after the departure of the two friars, the Reverend Father Chapoüin, Provincial of the Recollect Fathers, a man of great piety, returned to Paris. Sieur Hoüel called on him, and narrated **what had** taken place refpecting the authority of Father du Verger, and **the** miffion he had given to the Recollect Fathers. After which narrative the Provincial Father proceeded to extol the plan, and to intereft himfelf with zeal in it, promifing to promote it with all his power, and adding that he had not before well comprehended the fubject of this miffion ; and it is to be believed that God infpired him more and more to profecute the matter. Subfequently he fpoke of it to Monfeigneur the Prince de Condé, and to all the cardinals and bifhops who were then affembled at Paris for the Seffion of the Eftates. All of them approved and commended the plan ; and to fhow that they were favorably difpofed towards it, they affured the Sieur Provincial that they would devife among them-felves and the members of the Court means for raifing a fmall fund, and that they would collect fome money for affifting four friars to be chofen, and who were then chofen for the execution of fo holy a work. And in order to facili-tate the undertaking, I vifited at the Eftates the cardinals and bifhops, and urgently reprefented to them the advantage and ufefulnefs which might one day refult, in order by my entreaties to move them to give, and caufe others who might be ftimulated by their example to give, contributions

butions and prefents, leaving all to their good will and judgment.

The **contributions** which were made for the expenfes of this expedition amounted to nearly fifteen hundred *livres,* **which** were put into my hands, and then employed, accord-**ing to the** advice and in the prefence of the Fathers, for the purchafe of what was neceffary, not only for the maintenance of the Fathers who fhould undertake the journey into New France, but alfo for their clothing, and the attire and ornaments neceffary for performing divine fervice. The friars were fent on in advance to Honfleur, where their embarkation was to take place.

Now the Fathers who were appointed for this holy enterprife were Father Denis[72] as commiffary, Jean d'Olbeau,[73] Jofeph le Caron, and Pacifique du Pleffis,[74] each of whom was moved by a holy zeal and ardor to make the journey, through God's grace, in order to fee if they might produce fome good fruit, and plant in thefe regions the ftandard of Jefus Chrift, determined to live and to die for His holy name, fhould it be neceffary to do fo and the occafion require it. Everything having been prepared, they provided themfelves with church ornaments, and we with what was neceffary for our voyage.

I left Paris the laft day of February to meet at Rouen our affociates, and reprefent to them the will of Monfeigneur the Prince, and alfo his defire that thefe good Fathers

fhould

---

[72] Denis Jamay. Sagard writes this name *Jamet.*

[73] Jean d'Olbeau. *Vide Hiftoire du Canada,* par Gabriel Sagard, Paris, 1636. Trofs ed., Vol. I, p. 28.

[74] Pacifique du Pleffis was a lay brother, although the title of Father is given to him by feveral early writers. *Vide citations by Laverdière in loc,* Quebec ed., Vol. IV, p. 7.

fhould make the journey, fince he recognized the fact that
the affairs of the country could hardly reach any perfection
or advancement, if God fhould not firft of all be ferved ; with
which our affociates were highly pleafed, promifing to affift
the Fathers to the extent of their ability, and provide them
with the fupport they might need.

The Fathers arrived at Rouen the **twentieth** of March
following, where we ftayed fome time. Thence we went to
Honfleur to embark, where we alfo ftayed fome days, waiting
for our veffel to be got ready, and loaded with the necef-
faries for fo long a voyage. Meanwhile preparations were
made in matters of confcience, fo that each one of us might
examine himfelf, and cleanfe himfelf from his fins by peni-
tence and confeffion, in order to celebrate the facrament
and attain a ftate of grace, fo that, being thereby freer in
confcience, we might, under the guidance of God, expofe
ourfelves to the mercy of the waves of the great and
perilous fea.

This done, we embarked on the veffel of the affociation,
which was of three hundred and fifty tons burden, and was
called the Saint Étienne, commanded by Sieur de Pont
Gravé. We departed from Honfleur on the twenty-fourth
day of Auguft,[48] in the above-mentioned year, and fet fail
with a very favorable wind. We continued on our voyage
without encountering ice or other dangers, through the
mercy of God, and in a fhort time arrived off the place
called *Tadouffac*, on the twenty-fifth day of May, when we
rendered

[48] Read April 24. It is obvious from Sagard fays *le 24 d'Auril.* *Vide Hif-*
the context that it could not be Auguft. *toire du Canada*, Trofs ed., Vol. I. p. 36.

rendered thanks to God for having conducted us fo favorably to the harbor of our deftination.

Then **we** began **to** fet men at work to fit up our barques
in order to go to Quebec, the place of our abode, and to the
great Falls of Saint Louis, the rendezvous of the favages,
who come there to traffic.

The barques having been fitted up, we went on board
with the Fathers, one of whom, named Father Jofeph,[56] defired, without ftopping or making any ftay at Quebec, to go
directly to the great Falls, where he faw all the favages and
their mode of life. This induced him to go and fpend the
winter in their country and that of other tribes who have a
fixed abode, not only in order to learn their language, but alfo
to fee what the profpect was of their converfion to Chriftianity. This refolution having been formed, he returned to Quebec the twentieth day of June[57] for fome church ornaments
and other neceffaries. Meanwhile I had ftayed at Quebec in
order to arrange matters relating to our habitation, as the
lodgings of the Fathers, church ornaments, the conftruction
of a chapel for the celebration of the mafs, as alfo the em-
ployment of perfons for clearing up lands. I embarked for
the Falls together with Father Denis,[58] who had arrived the
fame day from Tadouffac with Sieur de Pont Gravé.

As to the other friars, viz., Fathers Jean and Pacifique,[59]
they ftayed at Quebec in order to fit up their chapel and
arrange their lodgings. They were greatly pleafed at feeing
the place fo different from what they had imagined, which
increafed their zeal.

We

[56] The Recollect Father Jofeph le Caron.
[57] *Vide Laverdière in loco.*
[58] Father Denis Jamay.
[59] Jean d'Olbeau and Pacifique du Pleffis.

We arrived at the Rivière des Prairies, five leagues below the Falls of Saint Louis, whither the favages had come down. I will not attempt to fpeak of the pleafure which our Fathers experienced at feeing, not only fo long and large a river, filled with many fine iflands and bordered by a region apparently fo fertile, but alfo a great number of ftrong and robuft men, with natures not fo favage **as their** manners, nor as they acknowledged they had **conceived them** to be, and very different from what they had been given to **under-** ftand, owing to their lack of cultivation. I will not enter into a defcription of them, but refer the reader to what I have faid about them in my preceding books, printed in the year 1614.[20]

To continue my narrative : We met Father Jofeph, who was returning to Quebec in order to make preparations, and take what he needed for wintering in their country. This I did not think advifable at this feafon, but coun- felled him rather to fpend the winter at our fettlement as being more for his comfort, and undertake the journey when fpring came or at leaft in fummer, offering to accom- pany him, and adding that by doing fo he would not fail to fee what he might have feen by going, and that by returning and fpending the winter at Quebec he would have the fociety of his brothers and others who remained at the fettlement, by which he would be more profited than by ftaying alone among thefe people, with whom he could not, in my opinion, have much fatisfaction. Never- thelefs,

[20] This refers to the volume bearing date 1613, but which may not have been actually iffued from the prefs till 1614.

thelefs, in fpite of all that could be faid to him and all reprefentations, he would not change his purpofe, being urged by a godly zeal and love for this people, and hoping to make known to them their falvation.

His motive in undertaking this enterprife, as he ftated to us, was that he thought it was neceffary for him to go there not only in order to become better acquainted with the characteriftics of the people, but alfo to learn more eafily their language. In regard to the difficulties which it was reprefented to him that he would have to encounter in his intercourfe with them, he felt affured that he could bear and overcome them, and that he could adapt himfelf very well and cheerfully to the manner of living and the inconveniences he would find, through the grace of God, of whofe goodnefs and help he felt clearly affured, being convinced that, fince he went on His fervice, and fince it was for the glory of His name and the preaching of His holy gofpel that he undertook freely this journey, He would never abandon him in his undertaking. And in regard to temporal provifions very little was needed to fatisfy a man who demands nothing but perpetual poverty, and who feeks for nothing but heaven, not only for himfelf but alfo for his brethren, it not being confiftent with his rule of life to have any other ambition than the glory of God, and it being his purpofe to endure to this end all the hardfhips, fufferings, and labors which might offer.

Seeing him impelled by fo holy a zeal and fo ardent a charity, I was unwilling to try any more to reftrain him. Thus he fet out with the purpofe of being the firft to announce through His holy favor to this people the name

of

of God, having the great fatisfaction that an opportunity
prefented itfelf for fuffering fomething for the name and
glory of our Saviour Jefus Chrift.

As foon as I had arrived at the Falls, I vifited the people,
who were very defirous of feeing us and delighted at our
return. They hoped that we would furnifh them fome
of our number to affift them in their wars againft our
enemies, reprefenting to us that they could with difficulty
come to us if we fhould not affift them; for the Iroquois,
they faid, their old enemies, were always on the road
obftructing their paffage. Moreover I had conftantly promifed to affift them in their wars, as they gave us to underftand by their interpreter. Whereupon Sieur Pont Gravé
and myfelf concluded that it was very neceffary to affift
them, not only in order to put them the more under obligations to love us, but alfo to facilitate my undertakings and
explorations which, as it feemed, could only be accomplifhed
by their help, and alfo as this would be a preparatory ftep to
their converfion to Chriftianity.[91] Therefore I refolved to
go and explore their country and affift them in their wars, in
order to oblige them to fhow me what they had fo many
times promifed to do.

We accordingly caufed them all to affemble together, that
we might communicate to them our intention. When they
had heard it, they promifed to furnifh us two thoufand five
hundred and fifty men of war, who would do wonders, with
the underftanding that I with the fame end in view fhould
furnifh

[91] Our views of the war policy of Champlain are ftated at fome length in
Vol. I. pp. 189-193.

furnifh as many men as poffible. This I promifed to do, being very glad to fee them decide fo well. Then I proceeded to make known **to** them the methods to be adopted for fighting, in which they took efpecial pleafure, manifefting a strong hope of victory. Everything having been decided upon, we feparated with the intention of returning for the execution of our undertaking. But before entering upon this journey, which would require not lefs than three or four months, it feemed defirable that I fhould go to our fettlement to make the neceffary arrangements there for my abfence.

On the —— day of —— following I fet out on my return to the Rivière des Prairies.[92] While there with two canoes of favages I met Father Jofeph, who was returning from our fettlement with fome church ornaments for celebrating the holy facrifice of the mafs, which was chanted on the border of the river with all devotion by the Reverend Fathers Denis and Jofeph, in prefence of all the people, who were amazed at feeing the ceremonies obferved and the ornaments which feemed to them fo handfome. It was fomething which they had never before feen, for thefe Fathers were the firft who celebrated here the holy mafs.

To return and continue the narrative of my journey: I arrived at Quebec on the 26th, where I found the Fathers Jean and Pacifique in good health. They on their part did their duty at that place in getting all things ready. They celebrated the holy mafs, which had never been faid there before, nor had there ever been any prieft in this region.

                                             Having

[92] Laverdière thinks it probable that Champlain left the Falls of St. Louis on the 23d of June, and that the Holy Mafs was celebrated on the Rivière des Prairies on the 24th, the feftival of St John the Baptift.

Having arranged all matters at Quebec, I took with me two men and returned to the Rivière des Prairies, in order to go with the favages. I left Quebec on the fourth day of July, and on the eighth of the month while *en route* I met Sieur du Pont Gravé and Father Denis, who were returning to Quebec, and who told me that the favages had departed greatly difappointed at my not going with them; and that many of them declared that we were dead or had been taken by the Iroquois, fince I was to be gone only four or five days, **but** had been gone ten. This made them and even our own Frenchmen give up hope, fo much did they long to fee us again. They told me that Father Jofeph had departed with twelve Frenchmen, who had been furnifhed to affift the favages. This intelligence troubled me fomewhat; fince, if I had been there, I fhould have arranged many things for the journey, which I could not now do. I was troubled not only on account of the fmall number of men, but alfo becaufe there were only four or five who were acquainted with the handling of arms, while in fuch an expedition the beft are not too good in this particular. All this however did not caufe me to lofe courage at all for going on with the expedition, on account of the defire I had of continuing my explorations. I feparated accordingly from Sieurs du Pont Gravé and Father Denis, determined to go on in the two canoes which I had, and follow after the favages, having provided myfelf with what I needed.

On the 9th of the month I embarked with two others, namely, one of our interpreters[*] and my man, accompanied

by

[*] This interpreter was undoubtedly Étienne Brûlé. It was a clearly defined policy of Champlain to fend fuitable young men among the favages, particularly

by ten favages in the two canoes, thefe being all they could
carry, as they were heavily loaded and encumbered with
clothes, which prevented me from taking more men.

We continued our voyage up the River St. Lawrence fome
fix leagues, and then went by the Rivière des Prairies,
which difcharges into that river. Leaving on the left the
Falls of St. Louis, which are five or fix leagues higher up,
and paffing feveral fmall falls on this river, we entered a lake,[94]
after paffing which we entered the river where I had been
before, which leads to the Algonquins,[95] a diftance of eighty-
nine leagues[96] from the Falls of St. Louis. Of this river I
have made an ample defcription, with an account of my
explorations, in my preceding book, printed in 1614.[97] For
this reafon I fhall not fpeak of it in this narrative, but pafs
on directly to the lake of the Algonquins.[99] Here we entered a river[99] which flows into this lake, up which we went
fome thirty-five leagues, paffing a large number of falls both
by land and water, the country being far from attractive, and
covered with pines, birches, and fome oaks, being alfo very
rocky, and in many places fomewhat hilly. Moreover it was
very barren and fterile, being but thinly inhabited by certain
Algonquin favages, called *Otaguottouemin*,[100] who dwell in
the

---

larly to learn their language, and fubfequently to act as interpreters. Brûlé
is fuppofed to have been of this clafs.

[94] The Lake of Two Mountains.

[95] The River Ottawa, which Champlain had explored in 1613, as far as
Allumet Ifland, where a tribe of the
Algonquins refided, called later *Kiche-
fipirini*. *Vide Relation des Jéfuites*,
1650, p. 34.

[96] This is an over-eftimate.

[97] Champlain here again, *Vide* note

99, refers to the iffue bearing date 1613.
It is not unlikely that while it bears the
imprint of 1613, it did not actually iffue
from the prefs till 1614.

[98] The lake or expanfion of the Ottawa
on the fouthern fide of Allumet Ifland
was called the lake of the Algonquins,
as Allumet Ifland was oftentimes called
the Ifland of the Algonquins.

[99] The River Ottawa.

[100] Père Vimont calls this tribe *Kota-
kouteuemi*. *Relation des Jéfuites*, 1640,
p. 34.

the country, and live by hunting and the fish they catch in
the rivers, ponds, and lakes, with which the region is well
provided. It seems indeed that God has been pleased to
give to these forbidding and desert lands some things in
their season for the refreshment of man and the inhabitants
of these places. For I assure you that there are along the
rivers many strawberries, also a marvellous quantity of blueberries,[101] a little fruit very good to eat, and other small
fruits. The people here dry these fruits for the winter, as
we do plums in France for Lent. We left this river, which
comes from the north,[102] and by which the savages go to the
Saguenay to barter their furs for tobacco. This place is
situated in latitude 46°, and is very pleasant, but otherwise
of little account.[103]

Continuing our journey by land, after leaving the river of
the Algonquins, we passed several lakes [104] where the savages
carry their canoes, and entered the lake of the Nipissings,[105]
in latitude 46° 15′, on the twenty-sixth day of the month,
having

p 34. Père Ragueneau gives *Outaoube-
touemiouek*, and remarks that their language is a mixture of Algonquin and
Montagnais. *Vide Relation des Jésuites*,
1650, p. 34; also *Laverdière in loco*.

[101] *Blués*, blueberries. The Canada
blueberry. *Vaccinium Canadense*. Under
the term *blués* several varieties may have
been included. Charlevoix describes
and figures this fruit under the name
*Bluet du Canada. Vide Description des
Plantes Principales de l'Amérique Septentrionale*. In *Histoire de la Nouvelle
France*, Paris, 1744. Tom. IV. pp. 371,
372; also Vol. I. p. 303, note 73, of this
work.

[102] At its junction with the Mattawan,
the Ottawa's course is from the north.

What is known as its east branch rises
150 miles north of the city of Ottawa.
Extending towards the west in a winding
course for the distance of about 300
miles, it turns towards the southeast,
and a few miles before it joins the Mattawan its course is directly south. From
its northeastern source by a short portage is reached the river Chomouchouan,
an affluent of Lake St. John and the
Saguenay.

[103] Mattawa is 197 miles from Ottawa.
We have no means of giving the latitude
with entire accuracy, but it is about
46° 20′.

[104] Lac du Talon and Lac la Tortue.

[105] Nipissings, or Nipissirini. Champlain writes *Nipisierinii*.

having gone by land and the lakes twenty-five leagues, or thereabouts.[106] We then arrived at the cabins of the savages, with whom we stayed two days. There was a large **number** of them, who gave us a very welcome reception. They are a people who cultivate the land but little. A shows the dress of these people as they go to war; B that of the women, which differs in no wise from that of the Montagnais and the great people of the Algonquins, extending far into the interior.[107]

During the time that I was with them the chief of this tribe and their most prominent men entertained us with many banquets according to their custom, and took the trouble to go fishing and hunting with me, in order to treat me with the greatest courtesy possible. These people are very numerous, there being from seven to eight hundred souls, who live in general near the lake. This contains a large number of very pleasant islands, among others one more than six leagues long, with three or four fine ponds and a number of fine meadows; it is bordered by very fine woods, that contain an abundance of game, which frequent the little ponds, where the savages also catch fish. The northern side of the lake is very pleasant, with fine meadows for the grazing of cattle, and many little streams, discharging into the lake.

They were fishing at that time in a lake very abundant in various kinds of fish, among others one a foot long that was
very

---

[106] On the 26th of July. The distance from the junction of the Ottawa and the Mattawan to Lake Nipissing is about thirty-two miles. If *lieues* were translated miles, it would be a not very incorrect estimate.

[107] *Vide* the representations here referred to.

very good. There are also other kinds which the savages catch for the purpose of drying and storing away. The lake is some eight leagues broad and twenty-five long,[108] into which a river[109] flows from the northwest, along which they go to barter the merchandise, which we give them in exchange for their peltry, with those who live on it, and who support themselves by hunting and fishing, their country containing great quantities of animals, birds, and fish.[110]

After resting two days with the chief of the **Nipissings** we re-embarked in our canoes, and entered a river, by which this lake discharges itself.[111] We proceeded down it some thirty-five leagues, and descended several little fails by land and by water, until we reached Lake Attigouautan. All this region is still more unattractive than the preceding, for I saw along this river only ten acres of arable land, the rest being rocky and very hilly. It is true that near Lake Attigouautan we found some Indian corn, but only in small quantity. Here our savages proceeded to gather some squashes, which were acceptable to us, for our provisions began to give out in consequence of the bad management of the savages, who ate so heartily at the beginning that towards the end very little was left, although we had only one meal a day. But, as I have mentioned before, we did not lack for blueberries[112] and strawberries; otherwise we should have been in danger of being reduced to straits.

We met three hundred men of a tribe we named *Cheveux*
Relevés,

---

[108] Lake Nipissing, whose dimensions are over-stated.

[109] Sturgeon River.

[110] Père Vimont gives the names of these tribes as follows,— *Timiscimi,* *Outimagami, Ouachegami, Mitchitamou, Outurbi, Kiristinon. Vide Relation des Jésuites.* 1640. p. 34.

[111] French River.

[112] *Blues. Vide antea,* note 101.

Relevés,[113] since their hair is very high and carefully arranged, and better dressed beyond all comparison than that of our courtiers, in spite of their irons and refinements. This gives **them a** handsome appearance. They have no breeches, **and** their bodies are very much pinked in divisions of various shapes. They paint their faces in various colors, have their nostrils pierced, and their ears adorned with beads. When they go out of their houses they carry a club. I visited them, became somewhat acquainted, and formed a friendship with them. I gave a hatchet to their chief, who was as much pleased and delighted with it as if I had given him some rich present. Entering into conversation with him, I inquired in regard to the extent of his country, which he pictured to me with coal on the bark of a tree. He gave me to understand that he had come into this place for drying **the** fruit called *blués*,[114] to serve for manna in winter, and when they can find nothing else. A and C show the manner in which they arm themselves when they go to war. They have as arms only the bow and arrow, made in the manner you see depicted, and which they regularly carry; also a round shield of dressed leather[115] made from an animal like the buffalo.[116]

The next day we separated, and continued our course along the shore of the lake of the Attigouautan,[117] which
contains

---

[113] This significant name is given with reference to their mode of dressing their hair.

[114] Blueberries, *Vaccinium Canadense*.

[115] *De cuir bouilly*, for *cuir bouilli*, literally "boiled leather."

[116] The shields of the savages of this region may have been made of the hide of the buffalo, although the range of this animal was far to the northwest of them. Champlain saw undoubtedly among the Hurons skins of the buffalo. *Vide postea*, note 180.

[117] Lake Huron is here referred to.

contains a large number of iflands. We went fome forty-
five leagues, all the time along the fhore of the lake. It is
very large, nearly four hundred leagues long from eaft to
weft, and fifty leagues broad, and in view of its great extent
I have named it the *Mer Douce.*[115] It is very abundant in
various forts of very good fifh, both thofe which we have and
thofe **we** do not, but efpecially in trout, which are enor-
moufly large, fome of which I faw as **long as four feet** and
a half, the leaft being two feet and **a half. There are alfo**
pike of like fize, and a certain kind of fturgeon, **a very large**
fifh and of remarkable excellence. The country bordering
this lake is partly hilly, as on the north fide, and partly flat,
inhabited by favages, and thinly covered with wood, including oaks. After croffing a bay, which forms one of **the**
extremities of the lake,[116] we went fome feven leagues until
we arrived in the country of the Attigouautan at a village
called *Otoüacha*, on the firft day of Auguft. Here we found
a great change in the country. It was here very fine, the
largeft part being cleared up, and many hills and feveral rivers rendering the region agreeable. I went to fee their Indian
corn, which was at that time far advanced for the feafon.

Thefe

[115] The greateft length of Lake Huron on a curvilinear line, between the dif-charge of St. Mary's Strait and the out-let, is about 240 miles; its length due north and fouth is 186 miles, and its ex-treme breadth about 220 miles. *Bou-chette.*

[116] Coafting along the eaftern fhore of the Georgian Bay, when they arrived at Matchedafh Bay they croffed it in a fouthwefterly courfe and entered the country of the Attigouautans, or, as they are fometimes called, the Attiguaouan-tans. *Relation des Jéfuites*, 1640, p. 78.

They were a principal tribe of the Hurons, living within the limits of the prefent county of Simcoe. It is to be regretted that the Jefuit Fathers did not accompany their relations with local maps by which we could fix, at leaft approximately, the Indian towns which they vifited, and with which they were fo familiar. For a defcription of the Hurons and of their country, the origin of the name and other interefting par-ticulars, *vide Pere Hierofme Lalemant, Relation des Jéfuites*, 1639, Quebec ed. p. 50.

These localities feemed to me very pleafant, in comparifon with fo difagreeable a region as that from which we had
come. **The next** day I went to another village, called *Car-*
***maron*, a** league diftant from this, where they received us in
a very friendly manner, making for us a banquet with their
bread, fquafhes, and fifh. As to meat, that is very fcarce
there. The chief of this village earneftly begged me to ftay,
to which I could not confent, but returned to our village,
where on the next night but one, as I went out of the cabin
to efcape the fleas, of which there were large numbers and
by which we were tormented, a girl of little modefty came
boldly to me and offered to keep me company, for which
I thanked her, fending her away with gentle remonftrances,
and fpent the night with fome favages.

The next day I departed from this village to go to another, called *Touaguainchain*, and to another, called *Tequé-*
nonquiaye, in which we were received in a very friendly
manner by the inhabitants, who fhowed us the beft cheer
they could with their Indian corn ferved in various ftyles.
This country is very fine and fertile, and travelling through
it is very pleafant.

Thence I had them guide me to Carhagouha, which was
fortified by a triple palifade of wood thirty-five feet high for
its defence and protection. In this village Father Jofeph
was ftaying, whom we faw and were very glad to find well.
He on his part was no lefs glad, and was expecting nothing
fo little as to fee me in this country. On the twelfth day of
Auguft the Recollect Father celebrated the holy mafs, and
a crofs was planted near a fmall houfe apart from the village,
which the favages built while I was ftaying there, awaiting
the

the arrival of our men and their preparation to go **to the**
war, in which they had been for a long time engaged.

Finding that they were fo flow in affembling their army,
and that I fhould have time to vifit their country, I refolved
to go by fhort days' journeys from village to village as far as
Cahiagué, where the rendezvous of the entire army was to
be, and which was fourteen leagues diftant from Carhagouha,
from which village I fet out on the **fourteenth** of Auguft
with ten of my companions. I vifited five of the more **im-**
portant villages, which were enclofed with palifades **of wood,**
and reached Cahiagué, the principal village of the country,
where there were two hundred large cabins and where all
the men of war were to affemble. Now in all thefe villages
they received us very courteoufly with their fimple welcome.
All the country where I went contains fome twenty to
thirty leagues, is very fine, and fituated in latitude 44° 30′.
It is very extenfively cleared up. They plant in it a great
quantity of Indian corn, which grows there finely. They
plant likewife fquafhes,[119] and fun-flowers,[121] from the feed of
which they make oil, with which they anoint the head. The
region is extenfively traverfed with brooks, difcharging into
the lake. There are many very good vines[120] and plums,

which

---

[119] *Sitrouilles* for *citrouilles. Vide*
Vol. II. p. 64, note 128.

[121] *Herbe au foleil.* The funflower of
Northeaft America, *Helianthus multi-
florus.* This fpecies is found from
Quebec to the Safkatchewan, a tributary
of Lake Winnipeg. *Vide Chronological
Hiftory of Plants,* by Charles Pickering,
M.D., Bofton, 1879. p. 914. Charlevoix, in the defcription of his journey
through Canada in 1720, fays: " The
Soleil is a plant very common in the
fields of the favages, and which grows
feven or eight feet high. Its flower,
which is very large, is in the fhape of
the marigold, and the feed grows in the
fame manner. The favages, by boiling
it, draw out an oil, with which they
greafe their hair." *Letters to the Dutchefs
of Lefdiguieres,* London, 1763, p. 95.

[120] *Vignes.* Probably the froft grape,
Vitis cordifolia.

which are excellent,[123] raſpberries,[124] ſtrawberries.[125] little wild apples,[126] nuts,[127] and a kind of fruit of the form and color of ſmall **lemons**, with a ſimilar taſte, but having an interior which is very good and almoſt like that of figs. The plant which bears this fruit is two and a half feet high, with but three or four leaves at moſt, which are of the ſhape of thoſe of the fig-tree, and each plant bears but two pieces of fruit. There are many of theſe plants in various places, the fruit being very good and ſavory.[128] Oaks, elms, and beeches [129] are numerous here, as alſo foreſts of fir, the regular retreat of partridges[130] and hares.[131] There are alſo quantities of ſmall cherries [132] and black cherries,[133] and the ſame varieties of wood that we have in our foreſts in France. The ſoil ſeems to me indeed a little ſandy, yet it is

for

[123] *Prunes.* The Canada plum, *Prunus Americana.*

[124] *Framboiſes.* The wild red raſpberry. *Rubus ſtrigoſus.*

[125] *Fraiſes.* The wild ſtrawberry, *Fragaria Virginiana. Vide Pickering Chro. Hist. Plants,* p. 771.

[126] *Petites pommes ſauvages.* Probably the American crab-apple, *Pyrus coronaria.*

[127] *Noix.* This may include the butternut and ſome varieties of the walnut. *Vide* Vol. I. p. 264.

[128] Doubtleſs the May-apple, *Podophyllum peltatum.* In the wilds of Simcoe this fruit may have ſeemed tolerable from the abſence of others more deſirable. Gray ſays, " It is ſlightly acid, mawkiſh, eaten by pigs and boys." Cf. *Florula Boſtonienſis,* by Jacob Bigelow, M.D. Boſton, 1824. pp. 215, 216.

[129] *Les Cheſnes, ormeaux, & heſtres.* For oaks ſee Vol. I. p. 264. Elms, plainly the white elm, *Ulmus Ameri-*

cana, so called in contradiſtinction to the red or ſlippery elm, *Ulmus fulva.* The ſavages ſometimes uſed the bark of the ſlippery elm in the conſtruction of their canoes when the white birch could not be obtained. *Vide Charlevoix's Letters,* 1763, p. 94. For the beech, ſee Vol. I. p. 264.

[130] *Perdrix.* Canada Grouſe, *Tetras Canadenſis,* ſometimes called the Spruce Partridge, differing from the partridge of New England, which is the Ruffed Grouſe, *Bonaſa umbellus.* This latter ſpecies is, however, found likewiſe in Canada.

[131] *Laſins.* The American hare. *Lepus Americanus.*

[132] *Ceriſes petites.* Reference is evidently here made to the wild red cherry, *Prunus Pennſ-lvanica,* which is the ſmalleſt of all the native ſpecies. *Cf.* Vol. I. p. 264.

[133] *Meriſes.* The wild black cherry. *Prunus ſerotina.*

for all that good for their kind of cereal. The small tract of country which I vifited is thickly fettled with a countlefs number of human beings, not to fpeak of the other diftricts where I did not go, and which, according to general report, are as thickly fettled or more fo than thofe mentioned above. I reflected what a great misfortune it is that fo many poor creatures live and die without the knowledge of God, and even without any religion or law eftablifhed among them, whether divine, political, or civil; for they neither worfhip, nor pray to any object, at leaft fo far as I could perceive from their converfation. But they have, however, fome fort of ceremony, which I fhall defcribe in its proper place, in regard to the fick, or in order to afcertain what is to happen to them, and even in regard to the dead. Thefe, however, are the works of certain perfons among them, who want to be confidentially confulted in fuch matters, as was the cafe among the ancient pagans, who allowed themfelves to be carried away by the perfuafions of magicians and diviners. Yet the greater part of the people do not believe at all in what thefe charlatans do and fay. They are very generous to one another in regard to provifions, but otherwife very avaricious. They do not give in return. They are clothed with deer and beaver fkins, which they obtain from the Algonquins and Nipiffings in exchange for Indian corn and meal.

On the 17th of Auguft I arrived at Cahiagué, where I was received with great joy and gladnefs by all the favages of the country, who had abandoned their undertaking, in the belief that they would fee me no more, and that the Iroquois had captured me, as I have before ftated. This was the

caufe of the great delay experienced in this expedition, they
even having poftponed it to the following year. Meanwhile
they received intelligence that a certain nation of their
allies,[184] dwelling three good days' journeys beyond the Entouhonorons,[185] on whom the Iroquois alfo make war, defired
to affift them in this expedition with five hundred good men;
alfo to form an alliance and eftablifh a friendfhip with us,
that we might all engage in the war together; moreover
that they greatly defired to fee us and give expreffion to the
pleafure they would have in making our acquaintance.

I was glad to find this opportunity for gratifying my
defire of obtaining a knowledge of their country. It is fituated only feven days from where the Dutch[186] go to traffic
on the fortieth degree. The favages there, affifted by the
Dutch, make war upon them, take them prifoners, and
cruelly put them to death; and indeed they told us that the
preceding

[184] The Carantouanais. *Vide Carte
de la Nouvelle France*, 1632, alfo Vol.
I. p. 304. This tribe was probably fituated on the upper waters of the Sufquehanna, and confequently fouth of
the Five Nations, although we faid in-
advertently in Vol. I. p. 128 that they
were on the weft of them. General
John S. Clark thinks their village was
at Waverly, near the border of Pennfyl-
vania. In Vol. I. p. 143 in the 15th line
from the top, we fhould have faid the
Carantouanais inftead of *Entouhonorons*.

[185] The Entouhonorons were a part, it
appears, of the Five Nations. Champlain fays they unite with the Iroquois
in making war againft all the other tribes
except the Neutral Nation. Lake Ontario is called *Lac des Entouhonorons*,
and Champlain adds that their country

is near the River St. Lawrence, the
paffage of which they forbid to all other
tribes. *Vide* Vol. I. pp. 303, 304. He
thus appears to apply the name *Iroquois* to the eaftern portion of the Five
Nations, particularly thofe whom he
had attacked on Lake Champlain; and
the Huron name, *Entouhonorons*, to the
weftern portion. The fubdivifions, by
which they were diftinguifhed at a later
period, were probably not then known,
at leaft not to Champlain.

[186] *Flament.* The Dutch were at
this time on the Hudfon, engaged in
the fur trade with the favages. *Vide
Hiftory of the State of New York* by
John Romeyn Brodhead, New York,
1853, pp. 58-65. *Hiftory of New Nether-
land* or *New York under the Dutch*, by
E. B. O'Callaghan, New York, 1846,
pp. 67-77.

preceding year, while making war, they captured three **of the**
Dutch, who were affifting their enemies,[137] as we do the **Atti-**
gouautans, and while in action one of their own men was
killed. Neverthelefs they did not fail to fend back the three
Dutch prifoners, without doing them any harm, fuppofing
that they belonged to our party, fince they had no knowledge
of us except by hearfay, never having feen a Chriftian; otherwife, they faid, thefe three prifoners would not have got off fo
eafily, and would not efcape again fhould they furprife **and**
take them. This nation is very warlike, as thofe of the nation
of the Attigouautans maintain. They have only three villages, which are in the midft of more than twenty others, on
which they make war without affiftance from their friends;
for they are obliged to pafs through the thickly fettled country of the Chouontouaroüon,[138] or elfe they would have to
make a very long circuit.

After arriving at the village, it was neceffary for me to
remain until the men of war fhould come from the furround-
ing villages, fo that we might be off as foon as poffible.
During this time there was a conftant fucceffion of banquets
and dances on account of the joy they experienced at feeing
me fo determined to affift them in their war, juft as if they
were already affured of victory.

The greater portion of our men having affembled, we fet
out from the village on the firft day of September, and paffed
along the fhore of a fmall lake,[129] diftant three leagues from
the village, where they catch large quantities of fifh, which
they

---

[137] Their enemies were the Iroquois.
[138] *Chouontouarouon*, another name for *Entouhonorons*.

[139] Lake Couchiching, a fmall fheet of water into which pafs by a fmall out-let the waters of Lake Simcoe.

they preserve for the winter. There is another lake,[140] closely adjoining, which is twenty-five leagues in circuit, and flows into the small one by a strait, where the above mentioned extensive fishing is carried on. This is done by means of a large number of stakes which almost close the strait, only some little openings being left where they place their nets, in which the fish are caught. These two lakes discharge into the *Mer Douce*. We remained some time in this place to await the rest of our savages. When they were all assembled, with their arms, meal, and necessaries, it was decided to choose some of the most resolute men to compose a party to go and give notice of our departure to those who were to assist us with five hundred men, that they might join us, and that we might appear together before the fort of the enemy. This decision having been made, they dispatched two canoes, with twelve of the most stalwart savages, and also with one of **our** interpreters,[141] who asked me to permit him to make the journey, which I readily accorded, inasmuch as he was led to do so of his own will, and as he might in this way see their country and get a knowledge of the people living there. The danger, however, was not small, since it was necessary to pass through the midst of enemies. They set out on the 8th of the month, and on the 10th following there was a heavy white frost.

We continued our journey towards the enemy, and went some five or six leagues through these lakes,[142] when the savages

ages

---

[140] Lake Simcoe. Laverdière says the Indian name of this lake was *Ouentaronk*, and that it was likewise called *Lac aux Claies*.

[141] Etienne Brûlé. *Vide postea*. p. 208.

[142] *Dans ces lacs.* From Lake Chouchiching, coasting along the northeastern shore of Lake Simcoe, they would make five or six leagues in reaching a point nearest to Sturgeon Lake.

ages carried their canoes about ten leagues by land. We then came to another lake,[142] fix to feven leagues in length and three broad. From this flows a river which difcharges into the great lake of the Entouhonorons. After traverfing this lake we paffed a fall, and continuing our courfe down this river for about fixty-four leagues[143] entered the lake of the Entouhonorons, having paffed, on our way by land, five falls, fome being from four to five leagues long. We alfo paffed feveral lakes of confiderable fize, through which the river paffes. The latter is large and very abundant in good fifh.

It is certain that all this region is very fine and pleafant. Along the banks it feems as if the trees had been fet out for ornament in moft places, and that all thefe tracts were in former times inhabited by favages, who were fubfequently compelled to abandon them from fear of their enemies. Vines and nut-trees are here very numerous. Grapes mature, yet there is always a very pungent tartnefs which is felt remaining in the throat when one eats them in large quantities, arifing from defect of cultivation. Thefe localities are very pleafant when cleared up.

Stags and bears are here very abundant. We tried the hunt and captured a large number as we journeyed down. It was done in this way. They place four or five hundred favages in line in the woods, fo that they extend to certain points on the river; then marching in order with bow and

arrow

---

[142] Undoubtedly Sturgeon Lake.

[143] From their entrance of Sturgeon Lake to the point where they reached Lake Ontario, at the eaftern limit of Amherft Ifland, the diftance is, in its winding and circuitous courfe, not far from Champlain's eftimate, viz. fixty-four leagues. That part of the river above Rice Lake is the Otonabee; that below is known as the Trent.

arrow in hand, fhouting and making a great noife in order
to frighten the beafts, they continue to advance until they
come to the end of the point. Then all the animals between the point and the hunters are forced to throw themfelves into the water, as many at least as do not fall by the
arrows fhot at them by the hunters. Meanwhile the favages,
who are exprefsly arranged and pofted in their canoes along
the fhore, eafily approach the ftags and other animals, tired
out and greatly frightened in the chafe, when they readily
kill them with the fpear heads attached to the extremity of
a piece of wood of the fhape of a half pike. This is the
way they engage in the chafe; and they do likewife on the
iflands where there are large quantities of game. I took
efpecial pleafure in feeing them hunt thus and in obferving their dexterity. Many animals were killed by the fhot
of the arquebus, at which the favages were greatly furprifed. But it unfortunately happened that, while a ftag
was being killed, a favage, who chanced to come in range,
was wounded by a fhot of an arquebus. Thence a great
commotion arofe among them, which however fubfided
when fome prefents were given to the wounded. This is
the ufual manner of allaying and fettling quarrels, and, in
cafe of the death of the wounded, prefents are given to
the relatives of the one killed.

As to fmaller game there is a large quantity of it in its
feafon. There are alfo many cranes,[145] white as fwans, and
other varieties of birds like thofe in France.

We

---

[145] *Grues.* The white crane, *Grus Americanus.* Adult plumage pure white. *Coues's Key to North American Birds,* Bofton, 1872. p. 271. Charlevoix fays, "We have cranes of two colors, fome white and others *gris de lin,*" that is
a

We proceeded by fhort days' journeys as far as the **fhore** of the lake of the Entouhonorons, conftantly hunting **as** before mentioned. Here at its eaftern extremity, which is the entrance to the great River St. Lawrence, we made the traverfe, in latitude 43°,[146] where in the paffage there are very large beautiful iflands. We went about fourteen leagues in paffing to the fouthern fide of the lake towards the territory of the enemy.[147] The favages concealed all **their** canoes in the woods near the fhore. We went fome **four leagues** over a fandy ftrand, where I obferved a very pleafant **and** beautiful country, interfected by many little ftreams and two fmall rivers, which difcharge into the before-mentioned lake, alfo many ponds and meadows, where there was an endlefs amount of game, many vines, fine woods, and a large number of cheftnut trees, whofe fruit was ftill in the burr. The cheftnuts are fmall, but of a good flavor. The country is covered with forefts, which over its greater portion have not been cleared up. All the canoes being thus hidden, we left the border of the lake,[148] which is fome eighty leagues long and

---

a purple or lilac color. This latter fpecies is the brown crane, *Grus Cana-denfis.* "Plumage plumbeous gray." *Cafus. Vide Charlevoix's Letters,* Lon-don, 1763, p. 88.

[146] The latitude of the eaftern end of Amherft Ifland is about 44° 11'.

[147] This traverfe, it may be prefumed, was made by coafting along the fhore, as was the cuftom of the favages with their light canoes.

[148] It appears that, after making by eftimate about fourteen leagues in their bark canoes, and four by land along the fhore, they ftruck inland. Guided merely by the diftances given in the text, it is not poffible to determine with exactnefs at what point they left the lake. This arifes from the fact that we are not fure at what point the meafurement began, and the eftimated diftances are given, moreover, with very liberal margins. But the eighteen leagues in all would take them not very far from Little Salmon River, whether the eftimate were made from the eaftern end of Amherft Ifland or Simcoe Ifland, or any place in that immediate neighborhood. The natural features of the country, for four leagues along the coaft north of Little Salmon River, anfwer well to the defcription given in the text. The cheft-nut

and twenty-five wide.[145] The greater portion of its shores is inhabited by savages. We continued our course by land for about twenty-five or thirty leagues. In the space of four days we crossed many brooks, and a river which proceeds from a **lake** that discharges into that of the Entouhonorons.[146] This lake is twenty-five or thirty leagues in circuit, contains some fine islands, and is the place where our enemies, the Iroquois, catch their fish, in which it abounds.

On the 9th of the month of October our savages going out to reconnoitre met eleven savages, whom they took prisoners. They consisted of four women, three boys, one girl, and three men, who were going fishing and were distant some four leagues from the fort of the enemy. Now it is to be noted that one of the chiefs, on seeing the prisoners, cut off the finger of one of these poor women as a beginning of their usual punishment; upon which I interposed and reprimanded the chief, Iroquet, representing to him that it was not the act of a warrior, as he declared himself to be, to conduct himself with cruelty towards women, who have no defence but their tears, and that one should treat them with humanity on account of their helplessness and weakness; and I told him that on the contrary this act would be deemed to proceed from a base and brutal courage, and that if he committed any more of these cruelties he would not give me heart

nut and wild grape are still found there. *Vide MS. Letters of the Rev. James Croft, D.D., LL.D.,* and of *S. D. Smith, Esq.,* of Mexico, New York.

[145] Lake Ontario, or Lake of the Entouhonorons, is about a hundred and eighty miles long, and about fifty-five miles in its extreme width.

[146] The river here crossed was plainly Oneida River, flowing from Oneida Lake into Lake Ontario. The lake is identified by the islands in it. Oneida Lake is the only one in this region which contains any islands whatever, and consequently the river flowing from it must be that now known as Oneida River.

heart to affift them or favor them in the war. To which the only anfwer he gave me was that their enemies treated them in the fame manner, but that, fince this was difpleafing to me, he would not do anything more to the women, although he would to the men.

The next day, at three o'clock in the afternoon, we arrived before the fort[181] of their enemies, where the favages made fome fkirmifhes with each other, although **our** defign was not to difclofe ourfelves until the next day, which **however** the impatience of our favages would not permit, **both on** account of their defire to fee fire opened upon their enemies, and alfo that they might refcue fome of their own men who had become too clofely engaged, and were hotly preffed. Then I approached the enemy, and although I had only a few men, yet we fhowed them what they had never feen nor heard before ; for, as foon as they faw us and heard the arquebus fhots and the balls whizzing in their ears, they withdrew fpeedily to their fort, carrying the dead and wounded in this charge. We alfo withdrew to our main body, with five or fix wounded, one of whom died.

This done, we withdrew to the diftance of cannon range, out of fight of the enemy, but contrary to my advice and to what they had promifed me. This moved me to addrefs them very rough and angry words in order to incite them to do their duty, forefeeing that if everything fhould go according to their whim and the guidance of their council, their utter ruin would be the refult. Neverthelefs I did not fail to fend to them and propofe means which they fhould ufe in order to get poffeffion of their enemies.

Thefe

[181] For the probable fite of this fort, fee Vol. I. p. 130, note 83.

17

These were, to make with certain kinds of wood a *cavalier*, which should be higher than the palisades. Upon this were to be placed four or five of our arquebusiers, who should keep up a constant fire over their palisades and galleries, which were well provided with stones, and by this means dislodge the enemy who might attack us from their galleries. Meanwhile orders were to be given to procure boards for making a sort of mantelet to protect our men from the arrows and stones of which the savages generally make use. These instruments, namely the cavalier and mantelets, were capable of being carried by a large number of men. One mantelet was so constructed that the water could not extinguish the fire, which might be set to the fort, under cover of the arquebusiers who were doing their duty on the cavalier. In this manner, I told them, we might be able to defend ourselves so that the enemy could not approach to extinguish the fire which we should set to their ramparts.

This proposition they thought good and very seasonable, and immediately proceeded to carry it out as I directed. In fact the next day they set to work, some to cut wood, others to gather it, for building and equipping the cavalier and mantelets. The work was promptly executed and in less than four hours, although the amount of wood they had collected for burning against the ramparts, in order to set fire to them, was very small. Their expectation was that the five hundred men who had promised to come would do so on this day, but doubt was felt about them, since they had not appeared at the rendezvous, as they had been charged to do, and as they had promised. This greatly troubled our
savages;

favages; but feeing that they were fufficiently numerous **to** take the fort without other affiftance, and thinking for my part that delay, if not in all things at leaft in many, is prejudicial, I urged them to attack it, reprefenting to them that the enemy, having become **aware of their** force and our arms, which pierced whatever was proof againft arrows, had begun **to** barricade themfelves and cover **themfelves** with ftrong pieces of wood, with which they **were well** provided and their village filled. I told them that the **leaft delay was the** beft, fince the enemy had already ftrengthened **themfelves** very much; for their village was enclofed by four good palifades, which were made of great pieces of wood, interlaced with each other, with an opening of not more than half a foot between two, and which were thirty feet high, with galleries after the manner of a parapet, which they had furnifhed with double pieces of wood that were proof againft our arquebus fhots. Moreover it was near a pond where the water was abundant, and was well fupplied with gutters, placed between each pair of palifades, to throw out water, which they had alfo under cover infide, in order to extinguifh fire. Now this is the character of their fortifications and defences, which are much ftronger than the villages of the Attigouautan and others.

We approached to attack the village, our cavalier being carried by two hundred of the ftrongeft men, who put it down before the village at a pike's length off. I ordered three arquebufiers to mount upon it, who were well protected from the arrows and ftones that could be fhot or hurled at them. Meanwhile the enemy did not fail to fend a large number of arrows which did not mifs, and a great

many

many ftones, which they hurled from their palifades. Neverthelefs a hot fire of arquebufes forced them to diflodge and
abandon their galleries, in confequence of the cavalier which
uncovered them, they not venturing to fhow themfelves, but
fighting under fhelter. Now when the cavalier was carried
forward, inftead of bringing up the mantelets according to
order, including that one under cover of which we were
to fet the fire, they abandoned them and began to fcream at
their enemies, fhooting arrows into the fort, which in my
opinion did little harm to the enemy.

But we muft excufe them, for they are not warriors, and
befides will have no difcipline nor correction, and will do only
what they pleafe. Accordingly one of them fet fire incon-
fiderately to the wood placed againft the fort of the enemy,
quite the wrong way and in the face of the wind, fo that it
produced no effect.

This fire being out, the greater part of the favages began
to carry wood againft the palifades, but in fo fmall quantity
that the fire could have no great effect. There alfo arofe
fuch diforder among them that one could not underftand
another, which greatly troubled me. In vain did I fhout in
their ears and remonftrate to my utmoft with them as to the
danger to which they expofed themfelves by their bad
behavior, but on account of the great noife they made they
heard nothing. Seeing that fhouting would only burft my
head, and that my remonftrances were ufelefs for putting a
ftop to the diforder, I did nothing more, but determined
together with my men to do what we could, and fire upon
fuch as we could fee.

Meanwhile the enemy profited by our diforder to get
water

water and pour it fo abundantly that you would have faid
brooks were flowing through their fpouts, the refult **of**
which was that the fire was inftantly extinguifhed, while
they did not ceafe fhooting their arrows, which fell upon us
like hail. But the men on the cavalier killed and maimed
many. We were engaged in this combat about three
hours, in which two of our chiefs and leading warriors were
wounded, namely, one called *Ochateguain* and another *Orani*,
together with fome fifteen common warriors. **The others,**
feeing their men and fome of the chiefs wounded, now
began to talk of a retreat without farther fighting, in expectation of the five hundred men,[138] whofe arrival could not be
much delayed. Thus they retreated, a diforderly rabble.

Moreover the chiefs have in fact no abfolute control over
their men, who are governed by their own will and follow
their own fancy, which is the caufe of their diforder and the
ruin of all their undertakings; for, having determined upon
anything with their leaders, it needs only the whim of a
villain, or nothing at all, to lead them to break it off and
form a new plan. Thus there is no concert of action among
them, as can be feen by this expedition.

Now we withdrew into our fort, I having received two
arrow wounds, one in the leg, the other in the knee, which
caufed me great inconvenience, afide from the fevere pain.
When they were all affembled, I addreffed them fome words
of remonftrance on the diforder that had occurred. But
all I faid availed nothing, and had no effect upon them.
They replied that many of their men had been wounded like
myfelf,

[138] They were of the tribe called Carantouanais. *Vide antea,* note 134.

myfelf, fo that it would caufe the others much trouble and inconvenience to carry them as they retreated, and that it was not poffible to return again againft their enemies, as I told them it **was** their duty to do. They agreed, how-**ever, to** come; and, if they came, to make a fecond effort againft their enemies, and execute better what I might tell them than they had done in the paft. With this I had to content myfelf, to my great regret.

Herewith is indicated the manner in which they fortify their towns, from which reprefentation it may be inferred that thofe of their friends and enemies are fortified in like manner.

The next day there was a violent wind, which lafted two days, and was very favorable for fetting fire anew to the fort of the enemy which, although I urged them ftrongly, they were unwilling to do, as if they were afraid of getting the worft of it, and befides they pleaded their wounded as an excufe.

We remained in camp until the 16th of the month,[148] during which time there were fome fkirmifhes between the enemy and our men, who were very often furrounded by the former, rather through their imprudence than from lack of courage; for I affure you that every time we went to the charge it was neceffary for us to go and difengage them from the crowd, fince they could only retreat under cover of our arquebufiers, whom the enemy greatly dreaded and feared; for as foon as they perceived any one of the arque-bufiers they withdrew fpeedily, faying in a perfuafive manner
that

---

[148] This was in the month of October.

that we fhould not interfere in their combats, and that **their** enemies had very little courage to require us to affift them, with many other words of like tenor, in order to prevail upon us.

I have reprefented by figure E the manner in which they arm themfelves in going to war.

After fome days, feeing that the five hundred men did not come, they determined to depart, and enter upon their retreat as foon as poffible. They proceeded to make a kind of bafket for carrying the wounded, who are put into it **crowded up in** a heap, being bound and pinioned in fuch a manner that it is as impoffible for them to move as for an infant in its fwaddling clothes; but this is not without caufing the wounded much extreme pain. This I can fay with truth from my own experience, having been carried fome days, fince I could not ftand up, particularly on account of an arrow-wound which I had received in the knee. I never found myfelf in fuch a *gehenna* as during this time, for the pain which I fuffered in confequence of the wound in my knee was nothing in comparifon with that which I endured while I was carried bound and pinioned on the back of one of our favages; fo that I loft my patience, and as foon as I could fuftain myfelf, got out of this prifon, or rather *gehenna*.

The enemy followed us about half a league, though at a diftance, with the view of trying to take fome of thofe compofing the rear guard; but their efforts were vain, and they retired.

Now the only good point that I have feen in their mode of warfare is that they make their retreat very fecurely, placing all the wounded and aged in their centre, being

well

well armed on the wings and in the rear, and continuing
this order without interruption until they reach a place of
fecurity.

Their retreat was very long, being from twenty-five to
thirty leagues, which caufed the wounded much fatigue, as
also thofe who carried them, although the latter relieved
each other from time to time.

On the 18th day of the month there fell much fnow and
hail, accompanied by a ftrong wind, which greatly incom-
moded us. Neverthelefs we fucceeded in arriving at the
fhore of the lake of the Entouhonorons, at the place where
our canoes were concealed, which we found all intact, for we
had been afraid left the enemy might have broken them up.

When they were all affembled, and I faw that they were
ready to depart to their village, I begged them to take me to
our fettlement, which, though unwilling at first, they finally
concluded to do, and fought four men to conduct me.
Four men were found, who offered themfelves of their own
accord ; for, as I have before faid, the chiefs have no control
over their men, in confequence of which they are often
unable to do as they would like. Now the men having
been found, it was neceffary alfo to find a canoe, which was
not to be had, each one needing his own, and there being no
more than they required. This was far from being pleafant
to me, but, on the contrary greatly annoyed me, fince it led
me to fufpect fome evil purpofe, inafmuch as they had
promifed to conduct me to our fettlement after their war.
Moreover I was poorly prepared for fpending the winter
with them, or elfe fhould not have been concerned about
the matter. But not being able to do anything, I was
obliged

obliged to refign myfelf in patience. Now after **fome**
days I perceived that their plan was to keep me and **my**
companions, not only as a fecurity for themfelves, for
they feared their enemies, but alfo that I might liften to
what took place in their councils and affemblies, and determine what they fhould do in the future againft their enemies
for their fecurity and prefervation.

The next day, the 28th of the **month, they** began
to make preparations; fome to go **deer-hunting, others to**
hunt bears and beavers, others to go fifhing, others **to return**
to their villages. An abode and lodging were furnifhed me
by one of the principal chiefs, called *D'Arontal*, with whom I
already had fome acquaintance. Having offered me his cabin,
provifions, and accommodations, he fet out alfo for the deer-
hunt, which is efteemed by them the greateft and moft noble
one. After croffing, from the ifland,[134] the end of the lake,
we entered a river[135] fome twelve leagues in extent. They
then carried their canoes by land fome half a league, when
we entered a lake[136] which was fome ten or twelve leagues
in circuit, where there was a large amount of game, as
fwans,[137] white cranes,[138] *outardes*,[139] ducks, teal, fong-thrufh,[140]
larks,

[134] *Et après auoir trauerfé le bout
du lac de ladite ifle.* From this form of
expreffion this ifland would feem to have
been vifited before. But no particular
ifland is mentioned on their former
traverfe of the lake. It is impoffible to
fix with certainty upon the ifland referred
to. It may have been Simcoe or Wolf
Ifland, or fome other.

[135] Probably Cataraqui Creek. *Vide*
Vol. I. p. 136.

[136] Perhaps Loughborough Lake, or
the fyftem of lakes of which this is a part.

[137] *Cygnes,* fwans. Probably the Trum-
peter Swan, *Cygnus buccinator.* They
were efpecially found in Sagard's time
about Lake Nipiffing. "Mais pour des
Cignes, qu'ils appellent *Horhes,* il y
en a principalement vers les Epiceri-
nys." *Vide Le Grand Voyage au Pays
des Hurons* par Fr. Gabriel Sagard,
Paris, 1632, p. 303.

[138] *Grués blanches. Vide antea,* n. 145.

[139] *Houftardes. Vide antea,* note 32.

[140] *Mauuis,* Song-Thrufh. Doubtlefs
the Robin, *Turdus migratorius.*

18

larks,[141] fnipe,[142] geefe,[143] and feveral other kinds of fowl too numerous to mention. Of thefe I killed a great number, which ftood us in good ftead while waiting for the capture of **a deer.** From there we proceeded to a certain place fome ten **leagues** diftant, where our favages thought there were deer in abundance. Affembled there were fome twenty-five favages, who fet to building two or three cabins out of pieces of wood fitted to each other, the chinks of which they ftopped up by means of mofs to prevent the entrance of the air, covering them with the bark of trees.

When they had done this they went into the woods to a fmall foreft of firs, where they made an enclofure in the form of a triangle, clofed up on two fides and open on one. This enclofure was made of great ftakes of wood clofely preffed together, from eight to nine feet high, each of the fides being fifteen hundred paces long. At the extremity of this triangle there was a little enclofure, conftantly diminifhing in fize, covered in part with boughs and with only an opening of five feet, about the width of a medium-fized door, into which the deer were to enter. They were fo expeditious in their work, that in lefs than ten days they had their enclofure in readinefs. Meanwhile other favages had gone fifhing, catching trout and pike of prodigious fize, and enough to meet all our wants.

All preparations being made, they fet out half an hour before day to go into the wood, fome half a league from
the

141 *Alouettes,* larks. Probably the Brown Lark, *Anthus ludovicianus.* Found everywhere in North America.
142 *Becaffines.* Probably the American Snipe. *Gallinago Wilfonii.*

143 *Oyes,* geefe. The common Wild Goose, *Branta Canadenfis,* or it may include all the fpecies taken collectively. For the feveral fpecies found in Canada, *vide antea,* note 32.

the before-mentioned enclofure, feparated from each other fome eighty paces. Each had two flicks, which they ftruck together, and they marched in this order at a flow pace until they arrived at their enclofure. The deer hearing this noife flee before them until they reach the enclofure, into which the favages force them to go. Then they gradually unite **on** approaching the bay and opening of their triangle, the deer fkirting the fides until **they reach** the end, to which the favages hotly purfue them, with bow **and arrow** in hand ready to let fly. On reaching the end **of the tri-** angle they begin to fhout and imitate wolves,[164] which are numerous, and which devour the deer. The deer, hearing this frightful noife, are conftrained to enter the retreat by the little opening, whither they are very hotly purfued by arrow fhots. Having entered this retreat, which is fo well clofed and faftened that they can by no poffibility get out, they are eafily captured. I affure you that there is a fingular pleaf- ure in this chafe, which took place every two days, and was fo fuccefsful that, in the thirty-eight days[165] during which we were there, they captured one hundred and twenty deer, which they make good ufe of, referving the fat for winter, which they ufe as we do butter, and taking away to their homes fome of the flefh for their feftivities.

They have other contrivances for capturing the deer; as fnares, with which they kill many. You fee depicted oppofite the manner of their chafe, enclofure, and fnare.

Out

---

[164] *Les loups.* The American Wolf, *Lupus occidentalis.*

[165] The thirty-eight days during which they were there would include the whole period from the time they began to make their preparations on the 28th of October on the fhores of Lake Ontario till they began their homeward journey on the 4th of December. *Vide antea*, p. 137; *poftea*, p. 143.

Out of the skins they make garments. Thus you see how
we spent the time while waiting for the frost, that we might
return the more easily, since the country is very marshy.

When they first went out hunting, I lost my way in the
woods, having followed a certain bird that seemed to me
peculiar. It had a beak like that of a parrot, and was of the
size of a hen. It was entirely yellow, except the head which
was red, and the wings which were blue, and it flew by intervals like a partridge. The desire to kill it led me to pursue it from tree to tree for a very long time, until it flew
away in good earnest. Thus losing all hope, I desired to
retrace my steps, but found none of our hunters, who had
been constantly getting ahead, and had reached the enclosure.
While trying to overtake them, and going, as it seemed to
me, straight to where the enclosure was, I found myself lost
in the woods, going now on this side now on that, without
being able to recognize my position. The night coming on,
I was obliged to spend it at the foot of a great tree, and in
the morning set out and walked until three o'clock in the
afternoon, when I came to a little pond of still water. Here
I noticed some game, which I pursued, killing three or four
birds, which were very acceptable, since I had had nothing
to eat. Unfortunately for me there had been no sunshine
for three days, nothing but rain and cloudy weather, which
increased my trouble. Tired and exhausted I prepared to
rest myself and cook the birds in order to alleviate the hunger which I began painfully to feel, and which by God's
favor was appeased.

When I had made my repast I began to consider what
I should do, and to pray God to give me the will and
                                                    courage

courage to fuftain patiently my misfortune if I fhould **be** obliged to remain abandoned in this foreft without counfel or confolation except the Divine goodnefs and mercy, and at the fame time to exert myfelf to return to our hunters. Thus committing all to His mercy I gathered up renewed courage going here and there **all** day, without perceiving any foot-print or path, except thofe of wild beafts, of which I generally faw a good number. **I was** obliged to pafs here this night alfo. Unfortunately **I had forgotten to** bring with me a fmall compafs which would have put **me** on the right road, or nearly fo. At the dawn of day, after a brief repaft, I fet out in order to find, if poffible, fome brook and follow it, thinking that it muft of neceffity flow into the river on the border of which our hunters were encamped. Having refolved upon this plan, I carried it out fo well that at noon I found myfelf on the border of a little lake, about a league and a half in extent, where I killed fome game, which was very timely for my wants; I had likewife remaining fome eight or ten charges of powder, which was a great fatisfaction.

I proceeded along the border of this lake to fee where it difcharged, and found a large brook, which I followed until five o'clock in the evening, when I heard a great noife, but on carefully liftening failed to perceive clearly what it was. On hearing the noife, however, more diftinctly, I concluded that it was a fall of water in the river which I was fearching for. I proceeded nearer, and faw an opening, approaching which I found myfelf in a great and far-reaching meadow, where there was a large number of wild beafts, and looking to my right I perceived the river, broad and long.

I

I looked to fee if I could not recognize the place, and walking along on the meadow I noticed a little path where the favages carried their canoes. Finally, after careful obfervation, I recognized it as the fame river, and that I had gone that way before.

I paffed the night in better fpirits than the previous ones, fupping on the little I had. In the morning I re-examined the place where I was, and concluded from certain mountains on the border of the river that I had not been deceived, and that our hunters muft be lower down by four or five good leagues. This diftance I walked at my leifure along the border of the river, until I perceived the fmoke of our hunters, where I arrived to the great pleafure not only of myfelf but of them, who were ftill fearching for me, but had about given up all hopes of feeing me again. They begged me not to ftray off from them any more, or never to forget to carry with me my compafs, and they added: If you had not come, and we had not fucceeded in finding you, we fhould never have gone again to the French, for fear of their accufing us of having killed you. After this he[166] was very careful of me when I went hunting, always giving me a favage as companion, who knew how to find again the place from which he ftarted fo well that it was fomething very remarkable.

To return to my fubject: they have a kind of fuperftition in regard to this hunt; namely, they believe that if they fhould roaft any of the meat taken in this way, or if any of the fat fhould fall into the fire, or if any of the bones fhould be

---

[166] The author here refers to the chief D'Arontal, whofe gueft he was. *Vide antea*, p. 137. Cf. alfo Quebec ed. 1632, p. 928.

be thrown into it, they would not be able to capture **any** more deer. Accordingly they begged me to roaſt none **of** this meat, but I laughed at this and their way of doing. Yet, in order not to offend them, I cheerfully deſiſted, at leaſt in their preſence; though when they were out of ſight I took ſome of the beſt and roaſted it, attaching no credit to their ſuperſtitions. When I afterwards told them what I had done, they would not believe me, ſaying that they could not have taken any deer after the doing of ſuch a thing.

On the fourth day of December we ſet out from this place, walking on the river, lakes, and ponds, which were **frozen,** and ſometimes through the woods. Thus we went for nineteen days, undergoing much hardſhip and toil, both the ſavages, who were loaded with a hundred pounds, and myſelf, who carried a burden of twenty pounds, which in the long journey tired me very much. It is true that I was ſometimes relieved by our ſavages, but neverthelefs I ſuffered great diſcomfort. The ſavages, in order to go over the ice more eaſily, are accuſtomed to make a kind of wooden ſledge,[167] on which they put their loads, which they eaſily and ſwiftly

drag

[167] *Traineau de bois*, a kind of ſledge. The Indian's ſledge was made of two pieces of board, which, with his ſtone axe and perhaps with the aid of fire, he patiently manufactured from the trunks of trees. The boards were each about ſix inches wide and ſix or ſeven feet long, curved upward at the forward end and bound together by crofs pieces. The ſides were bordered with ſtrips of wood, which ſerved as brackets, to which was faſtened the ſtrap that bound the baggage upon the ſledge. The load was dragged by a rope or ſtrap of leather paſſing round the breaſt of the ſavage and attached to the end of the ſledge. The ſledge was ſo narrow that it could be drawn eaſily and without impediment wherever the ſavage could thread his way through the pathlefs foreſts.

The journey from their encampment northeaſt of Kingſton on Lake Ontario to the capital of the Hurons was not lefs in a ſtraight line than a hundred and ſixty miles. Without a pathway, in the heart of winter, through water and melting ſnow, with their heavy burdens, the hardſhip and exhauſtion can hardly be exaggerated.

drag along. Some days after there was a thaw, which caufed us much trouble and annoyance; for we had to go through pine forefts full of brooks, ponds, marfhes, and fwamps, where many trees had been blown down upon each **other.** This caufed us a thoufand troubles and embarraffments, and great difcomfort, as we were all the time wet to above our knees. We were four days in this plight, fince in moft places the ice would not bear. At laft, on the 20th of the month, we fucceeded in arriving at our village.[158] Here the Captain Yroquet had come to winter with his companions, who are Algonquins, alfo his fon, whom he brought for the fake of treatment, fince while hunting he had been ferioufly injured by a bear which he was trying to kill.

After refting fome days I determined to go and vifit Father Jofeph, and to fee in winter the people where he was, whom the war had not permitted me to fee in the fummer. I fet out from this village on the 14th[169] of January following, thanking my hoft for the kindnefs he had fhown me, and, taking formal leave of him, as I did not expect to fee him again for three months.

The next day I faw Father Jofeph,[170] in his fmall houfe where he had taken up his abode, as I have before ftated. I ftayed with him fome days, finding him deliberating about making a journey to the Petun people, as I had alfo thought

of

[158] Namely at Cahiagué. In the iffue of 1632, Champlain fays they arrived on the 23d day of the month. *Vide* Quebec ed., p. 029. Leaving on the 4th and travelling nineteen days, as ftated above, they would arrive on the 23d December.

[169] Probably the 4th of January.

[170] Father Jofeph Le Caron had remained at Carhagouha, during the abfence of the war party in their attack upon the Iroquois, where Champlain probably arrived on the 5th of January.

of doing, although it was very difagreeable travelling **in** winter. We fet out together on the fifteenth of February to go to that nation, where we arrived on the feventeenth of the month.[171] Thefe Petun people plant the maize, called by us *blé de Turquie*, and have fixed abodes like the reft. We went to feven other villages of their neighbors and allies, with whom we contracted friendfhip, and who prom- ifed to come in good numbers to our **fettlement**. They wel- comed us with good cheer, making a banquet **with** meat and fifh, as is their cuftom. To this the people **from** all quarters flocked in order to fee us, fhowing many manifef- tations of friendfhip, and accompanying us on the greater part of our way back. The country is diversified with pleafant flopes and plains. They were beginning to build two villages, through which we paffed, and which were fituated in the midft of the woods, becaufe of the conven- ience[172] of building and fortifying their towns there. Thefe people live like the Attignouaatitans,[173] and have the fame cuftoms. They are fituated near the Nation Neutre,[174] which

are

[171] In the iffue of 1632, the arrival of Champlain and Le Caron is ftated to have occurred on the 17th of January. This harmonizes with the correction of dates in notes 169, 170.

The Huron name of the Petuns was *Tionnontateronons*, or *K'hionontatero- nons*, or *Quieunontateronons*. Of them Vimont fays, "Les Khionontateronons, qu'on appelle la nation du Petun, pour l'abondance qu'il y a de cette herbe, font eloignez du pays des Hurons, dont ils parlent la langue, environ douze ou quinze lieues tirant à l'Occident." *Vide Relation des Jefuites*, 1640, p. 95 : *His. Du Canada*, Vol. I. p. 209. Sagard.

For fome account of the fubfequent hif- tory of the Nation de Petun, *vide In- dian Migration in Ohio*, by C. C. Bald- win, 1879, p. 2.

[172] It was of great importance to the Indians to felect a fite for their villages where fuitable wood was acceffible, both for fortifying them with palifades and for fuel in the winter. It could not be brought a great diftance for either of thefe purpofes. Hence when the wood in the vicinity became exhaufted they were compelled to remove and build anew.

[173] That is to fay like the Hurons.

[174] The Nation Neutre was called by the

are powerful and occupy a great extent of country. After
visiting these people, we set out from that place, and went
to a nation of savages, whom we named *Cheveux Relevés*,[175]
They were very happy to see us again, and we entered into
friendship with them, while they in return promised to come
and see us, namely at the habitation in this place.

It has seemed to me desirable to describe them and their
country, their customs and mode of life. In the first place
they are at war with another nation of savages, called Assista-
gueröüon,[176] which means *Gens de Feu*, who are distant from
them ten days' journey. I informed myself accordingly very
particularly in regard to their country and the tribes living
there, as also to their character and numbers. The people
of this nation are very numerous, and are for the most
part

the Hurons *Attistondaronk* or *Attihon-
andaron*. *Vide Relation des Jésuites*,
1641, p. 72: *Dictionaire de la Langve
Hvronne*, par Sagard, a Paris, 1632.
Champlain places them on his map of
1632 south of Lake Erie. His knowledge of that lake, obtained from the
savages, was very meagre as the map
itself shows. The Neutres are placed
by early writers on the west of Lake
Ontario and north of Lake Erie. *Vide
Laverdière in loco*, Quebec ed., p. 546;
also, *Indian Migration in Ohio*, by C.
C. Baldwin, p. 4. They are placed far
to the south of Lake Erie by Nicholas
Sanson. *Vide Cartes de l'Amerique*,
1657.

[175] The Cheveux Relevés are represented by Champlain as dwelling west
of the Petuns, and were probably not
far from the most southern limit of
the Georgian Bay. Strangely enough
Nicholas Sanson places them on a large
island that separates the Georgian Bay

from Lake Huron. *Vide Cartes de
l'Amerique* par N. Sanson, 1657.

[176] *Assistaehronons, en Nation du
Feu*. Their Algonquin name was Mas-
coutins or Maskoutens, with several
other orthographies. The significance
of their name is given by Sagard as follows: Ils sont errans, sinon que quel-
ques villages d'entr'eux sement des
bleds d'Inde, et font la guerre à une
autre Nation, nommée *Assistagueronon*,
qui veut dire gens de feu; car en langue
Huronne *Assista* signifie du feu, et
Eronon, signifie Nation. *Le Grand
Voyage du Pays des Hvrons*, par Gabriel
Sagard, a Paris, 1632, p. 78. *Vide
Relation des Jésuites*, 1641, p. 72; *Discovery and Exploration of the Missis-
sippi Valley*, by John Gilmary Shea, p.
13; *Indian Migration in Ohio*, by C.
C. Baldwin, pp. 9, 10; *Discovery of the
Northwest by John Nicolet*, by C. W.
Butterfield, p. 63; *L'Amerique en
Plusieurs Cartes*, par N. Sanson, 1657.

part great warriors, hunters, and fishermen. They **have** several chiefs, each ruling in his own diftrict. In general they plant Indian corn, and other cereals. They are hunters who go in troops to various regions and countries, where they traffic with other nations, diftant four or five hundred leagues. They are the cleaneft favages in their houfehold affairs that I have ever feen, and are very induftrious in making a kind of mat, which conftitutes their Turkifh carpets. The women have the body **covered, but** the men go uncovered, with the exception of a fur **robe** in the form of a cloak, which they ufually leave off in fummer. The women and girls are not more moved at feeing them thus, than if they faw nothing unufual. The women live very happily with their hufbands. They have the following cuftom when they have their catamenia: the wives withdraw from their hufbands, or the daughter from her father and mother and other relatives, and go to certain fmall houfes. There they remain in retirement, awaiting their time, without any company of men, who bring them food and neceffaries until their return. Thus it is known who have their catamenia and who have not. This tribe is accuftomed more than others to celebrate great banquets. They gave us good cheer and welcomed us very cordially, earneftly begging me to affift them againft their enemies, who dwell on the banks of the *Mer Douce,* two hundred leagues diftant; to which I replied that they muft wait until another time, as I was not provided with the neceffary means. They were at a lofs how to welcome us. I have reprefented them in figure C as they go to war.

There is, alfo, at a diftance of a two days' journey from them,

in

in a southerly direction, another savage nation, that produces
a large amount of tobacco. This is called *Nation Neutre.*
They number four thousand warriors, and dwell westward of
the lake **of the** Entouhonorons, which is from eighty to a
hundred leagues in extent. They, however, assist the *Cheveux Relevés* against the *Gens de Feu.* But with the Iroquois
and our allies they are at peace, and preserve a neutrality.
There is a cordial understanding towards both of these nations, and they do not venture to engage in any dispute or
quarrel, but on the contrary often eat and drink with them
like good friends. I was very desirous of visiting this nation,
but the people where we were dissuaded me from it, saying that the year **before** one of our men had killed one of
them, when we were at war with the Entouhonorons, which
offended them; **and** they informed us that they are much
inclined to revenge, not concerning themselves as to who
struck the blow, but inflicting the penalty upon the first one
they meet of the nation, even though one of their friends,
when they succeed in catching him, unless harmony has
been previously restored between them, and gifts and presents bestowed upon the relatives of the deceased. Thus I
was prevented for the time being from going, although some
of this nation assured us that they would do us no harm for
the reason assigned above.

Thus we were led to return the same way we had come,
and continuing my journey, I reached the nation of the
Pisierinii,[177] who had promised to conduct me farther on in

the

---

[177] *Pisierinii,* the Nipissings. This
relates to those Nipissings who had accompanied Champlain on the expedition
against the Iroquois, and who were pass-
ing the winter among the Hurons. He
had expected that they would accompany

the profecution of my plans and explorations. But **I was** prevented by the intelligence which came from our **great** village and the Algonquins, where Captain Yroquet was, namely, that the people of the nation of the Atignouaatitans [118] had placed in his hands a prifoner of a hoftile nation, in the expectation that this Captain Yroquet would exercife on the prifoner the revenge ufual among them. But they faid that, inftead of doing fo, he had not only **fet** him at liberty, but, having found him apt, and an excellent **hunter**, had treated him as his fon, on account of **which the Ati**gnouaatitans had become jealous and refolved upon vengeance, and had in fact appointed a man to go and kill this prifoner, allied as he was. As he was put to death in the prefence of the chiefs of the Algonquin nation, they, indignant at fuch an act and moved to anger, killed on the fpot this rafh murderer; whereupon the Atignouaatitans feeling themfelves infulted, feeing one of their comrades dead, feized their arms and went to the tents of the Algonquins, who were paffing the winter near the above mentioned village, and belabored them feverely, Captain Yroquet receiving two arrow wounds. At another time they pillaged fome of the cabins of the Algonquins before the latter could place themfelves in a ftate of defence, fo that they had not **an** equal chance. Notwithftanding this they were not reconciled to the Algonquins, who for fecuring peace had given the Atignouaatitans fifty necklaces of porcelain and a hundred

pany him on explorations on the north of them. But arriving at their encampment, or his return from the Petuns and Cheveux Relevés, he learned from them of the quarrel that had arifen between the Algonquins and the Hurons. [118] Attigouantans, the principal tribe of the Hurons.

dred branches of the fame [179] which they value highly, and
likewife a number of kettles and axes, together with two
female prifoners in place of the dead man. They were, in a
word, ftill in a ftate of violent animofity. The Algonquins
were obliged to fuffer patiently this great rage, and feared
that they might all be killed, not feeling any fecurity,
notwithftanding their gifts, until they fhould be differently
fituated. This intelligence greatly difturbed me, when I
confidered the harm that might arife not only to them, but
to us as well, who were in their country.

I then met two or three favages of our large village, who
earneftly entreated me to go to them in order to effect a
reconciliation, declaring that if I did not go none of them
would come to us any more, fince they were at war with the
Algonquins and regarded us as their friends. In view of
this I fet out as foon as poffible, and vifited on my way the
Nipiffings to afcertain when they would be ready for the
journey to the north, which I found broken off on account of
these quarrels and hoftilities, as my interpreter gave me to
underftand, who faid that Captain Yroquet had come among
all thefe tribes to find and await me. He had requefted
them to be at the habitation of the French at the fame time
with himfelf to fee what agreement could be made between
them and the Atignouaatitans, and to poftpone the journey
to the north to another time. Moreover, Yroquet had given
                                                   porcelain

---

[179] *Colliers de pourceline.* Thefe
necklaces were compofed of fhells,
pierced and ftrung like beads. They
were of a violet color, and were efteemed
of great value. The *branches* were
ftrings of white fhells, and were more
common and lefs valuable. An en-
graved reprefentation may be feen in
Hiftoire de L'Amerique Septentrionale,
par De la Potherie, Paris, 1722, Tom. I.
p. 334. For a full defcription of thefe
necklaces and their fignificance and ufe
in their councils, *vide Charlevoix's Letters,* London, 1763, p. 132.

porcelain to break off this journey. They promifed us **to be** at our habitation at the fame time as the others.

If ever there was one greatly difheartened it was myfelf, fince I had been waiting to fee this year what during many preceding ones I had been feeking for with great toil and effort, through fo many fatigues and rifks of my life. But realizing that I could not help the matter, and that every-thing depended on the will of God, I comforted myfelf, re-folving to fee it in a fhort time. I had fuch **fure** informa-tion that I could not doubt the report of thefe people, who go to traffic with others dwelling in thofe northern regions, a great part of whom live in a place very abundant in the chafe, and where there are great numbers of large animals, the fkins of feveral of which I faw, and which I concluded were buffaloes[180] from their reprefentation of their form. Fifhing is alfo very abundant there. This journey requires forty days, as well in returning as in going.

I fet out towards our above-mentioned village on the 15th of February, taking with me fix of our men. Having arrived at that place the inhabitants were greatly pleafed, as alfo the Algonquins, whom I fent our interpreter to vifit in order to afcertain how everything had taken place on both **fides,**

[180] *Buffles,* buffaloes. The American Bifon, *Bos Americanus.* The fkins feen by Champlain in the poffeffion of the favages feem to indicate that the range of the buffalo was probably far-ther eaft at that period than at the prefent time, its eaftern limit being now about the Red River, which flows into Lake Winnipeg. The limit of its northern range is generally ftated to be at latitude 60°, but it is fometimes found as far north as 63° or 64°. *Vide* Dr. Shea's interefting account of the buffalo in *Difcovery and Exploration of Miffiffippi Valley,* p. 18. The range of the Mufk Ox is ftill farther north, rarely fouth of latitude 67°. His home is in the Barren Grounds, weft of Hud-fon Bay, and on the iflands on the north of the American Continent, where he fubfifts largely on lichens and the meagre herbage of that frofty region.

fides, for I did not wish to go myself that I might give no ground for fufpicion to either party.

Two days were fpent in hearing from both fides how everything had taken place. After this the principal men **and** feniors of the place came away with us, and we all together went to the Algonquins. Here in one of their cabins, where feveral of the leading men were affembled, they all, after fome talk, agreed to come and accept all that might be faid by me as arbiter in the matter, and to carry out what I might propofe.

Then I gathered the views of each one, obtaining and inveftigating the wifhes and inclinations of both parties, and afcertained that all they wanted was peace.

I fet forth to them that the beft courfe was to become reconciled and remain friends, fince being united and bound together they could the more eafily withftand their enemies; and as I went away I begged them not to afk me to effect their reconciliation if they did not intend to follow in all re-fpects the advice I fhould give them in regard to this difpute, fince they had done me the honor to requeft my opinion. Whereupon they told me anew that they had not defired my return for any other reafon. I for my part thought that if I fhould not reconcile and pacify them they would feparate ill difpofed towards each other, each party thinking itfelf in the right. I reflected, alfo, that they would not have gone to their cabins if I had not been with them, nor to the French if I had not interefted myfelf and taken, fo to fpeak, the charge and conduct of their affairs. Upon this I faid to them that as for myfelf I propofed to go with my hoft, who had always treated me well, and that I could with difficulty

find

find one fo good; for it was on him that the Algonquins laid
the blame, faying that he was the only captain who had
caufed the taking up of arms. Much was faid by both fides,
and finally it was concluded that I fhould tell them what
feemed to me beft, and give them my advice.

Since I faw now from what was faid that they referred the
whole matter to my own decifion as to that of a father, and
promifed that in the future I might difpofe of them as I
thought beft, referring the whole matter to **my** judgment
for fettlement, I replied that I was very glad to fee them **fo**
inclined to follow my advice, and affured them that it fhould
be only for the beft interefts of the tribes.

Moreover I told them, I had been greatly difturbed at
hearing the further fad intelligence, namely the death of one
of their relatives and friends, whom we regarded as one of
our own, which might have caufed a great calamity refulting
in nothing but perpetual wars between both parties, with
various and ferious difafters and a rupture of their friendfhip, in confequence of which the French would be deprived
of feeing them and of intercourfe with them, and be obliged
to enter into alliance with other nations; fince we loved
each other as brothers, leaving to God the punifhment of
thofe meriting it.

I proceeded to fay to them, that this mode of action between two nations, who were, as they acknowledged, friendly
to each other, was unworthy of reafoning men, but rather
characteriftic of brute beafts. I reprefented to them, moreover, that they were enough occupied in repelling their
enemies who purfued them, in routing them as often as
poffible, in purfuing them to their villages and taking them
prifoners;

prisoners; and that these enemies, seeing divisions and wars among them, would be delighted and derive great advantage therefrom, and be led to lay new and pernicious plans, in the hope of soon being able to see their ruin, or at least their enfeebling through one another, which would be the truest and easiest way for them to conquer and become masters of their territories, since they did not assist each other.

I told them likewise that they did not realize the harm that might befall them from thus acting; that on account of the death of one man they hazarded the lives of ten thousand, and ran the risk of being reduced to perpetual slavery; that, although in fact one man was of great value, yet they ought to consider how he had been killed, and that it was not with deliberate purpose, nor for the sake of inciting a civil war, it being only too evident that the dead man had first offended, since with deliberate purpose he had killed the prisoner in their cabins, a most audacious thing, even if the latter were an enemy. This aroused the Algonquins, who, seeing a man that had been so bold as to kill in their own cabins another to whom they had given liberty and treated as one of themselves, were carried away with passion; and some, more excited than the rest, advanced, and, unable to restrain or control their wrath, killed the man in question. Nevertheless they had no ill feeling at all towards the nation as a whole, and did not extend their purposes beyond the audacious one, who, they thought, fully deserved what he had wantonly earned.

And besides I told them they must consider that the Entouhonoron, finding himself wounded by two blows in the stomach,

ftomach, tore from his wound the knife which his **enemy**
had left there and gave the latter two blows, as I had **been**
informed; fo that in fact one could not tell whether it was
really the Algonquins who had committed the murder. And
in order to fhow to the Attigouantans that the Algonquins
did not love the prifoner, and that Yroquet did not bear
towards him the affection which they were difpofed to think,
I reminded them that they had eaten him, as he had inflicted
blows with a knife upon his enemy; a thing, however, **un-**
worthy of a human being, but rather characteriftic of **brute**
beafts.

I told them alfo that the Algonquins very much regretted
all that had taken place, and that, if they had fupppofed fuch
a thing would have happened, they would have facrificed this
Iroquois for their fatisfaction. I reminded them likewife
that they had made recompenfe for this death and offence,
if fo it fhould be called, by large prefents and two prifoners,
on which account they had no reafon at prefent to complain, and ought to reftrain themfelves and act more mildly
towards the Algonquins, their friends. I told them that,
fince they had promifed to fubmit every thing to arbitration,
I entreated them to forget all that had paffed between them
and never to think of it again, nor bear any hatred or ill will
on account of it to each other, but to live good friends as
before, by doing which they would conftrain us to love them
and affift them as I had done in the paft. But in cafe they
fhould not be pleafed with my advice, I requefted them to
come, in as large numbers as poffible, to our fettlement, fo
that there, in the prefence of all the captains of veffels, our
friendfhip might be ratified anew, and meafures taken to
fecure

fecure them from their enemies, a thing which they ought
to confider.

Then they began to fay that I had fpoken well, and that
they would adhere to what I had faid, and all went away to
their cabins, apparently fatisfied, excepting the Algonquins,
who broke up and proceeded to their village, but who, as it
feemed to me, appeared to be not entirely fatisfied, fince
they faid among themfelves that they would not come to
winter again in thefe places, the death of thefe two men
having coft them too dearly. As for myfelf, I returned to
my hoft, in whom I endeavored to infpire all the courage I
could, in order to induce him to come to our fettlement,
and bring with him all thofe of his country.

During the winter, which lafted four months, I had fufficient leifure to obferve their country, cuftoms, drefs, manner
of living, the character of their affemblies, and other things
which I fhould like to defcribe. But it is neceffary firft to
fpeak of the fituation of the country in general and its divifions, alfo of the location of the tribes and the diftances
between them.

The country extends in length, in the direction from eaft
to weft, nearly four hundred and fifty leagues, and fome
eighty or a hundred leagues in breadth from north to fouth,
from latitude 41° to 48° or 49°.[151] This region is almoft an
ifland, furrounded by the great river Saint Lawrence, which
paffes through feveral lakes of great extent, on the fhores
of which dwell various tribes fpeaking different languages,
having fixed abodes, and all fond of the cultivation of the
foil, but with various modes of life, and cuftoms, fome better
than

---

[151] Champlain is here fpeaking of the whole country of New France.

than others. On the fhore north of this great river, extending wefterly fome hundred leagues towards the Attigouantans,[182] there are very high mountains, and the air is more
temperate than in any other part of thefe regions, the latitude
being 41°. All thefe places abound in game, fuch as ftags,
caribous, elks, does,[183] buffaloes, bears, wolves, beavers, foxes,
minxes,[184] weafels,[185] and many other kinds of animals which
we do not have in France. Fifhing is abundant, there being
many varieties, both thofe which we have in France, as
alfo others which we have not. There are likewife **many**
birds in their time and feafon. The country is traverfed by
numerous rivers, brooks, and ponds, connecting with each
other and finally emptying into the river St. Lawrence and
the lakes through which it paffes. The country is very
pleafant in fpring, is covered with extenfive and lofty forefts, and filled with wood fimilar to that which we have in
France, although in many places there is much cleared land,
where they plant Indian corn. This region alfo abounds in
meadows, lowlands, and marfhes, which furnifh food for the
animals before mentioned.

The country north of the great river is very rough and
mountainous, and extends in latitude from 47° to 49°, and
in places abounds in rocks.[186] So far as I could make out,
these

---

[182] This fentence in the original is
unfinifhed and defective. *Au cofté vers
le Nort, icelle grande riuiere tirant à
l'Occident*, etc. In the ed. 1632, the
reading is *Au cofté vers le nort d'icelle
grande riuiere tirant au furouft*, etc.
The tranflation is according to the ed.
of 1632. *Vide* Quebec ed., p. 941.

[183] Champlain here gives the four

species of the *cervus* family under
names then known to him, viz., the
moofe, wapiti or elk, caribou, and the
common deer.

[184] *Foſſines*, a quadruped known as
the minx or mink. *Muſtela viſon*.

[185] *Martes*, weafels, *Muſtela vulgaris*.

[186] *The country on the north*, &c.
Having defcribed the country along the
coaft

thefe regions are inhabited by favages, who wander through the country, not engaging in the cultivation of the foil, nor doing anything, or at leaft as good as nothing. But **they are** hunters, now in one place, now in another, the **region** being very cold and difagreeable. This land on the **north is** in latitude 49° and extends over fix hundred leagues in breadth from eaft to weft, of parts of which we have full knowledge. There are alfo many fine large rivers rifing in this region and difcharging into the before-mentioned river, together with an infinite number of fine meadows, lakes, and ponds, through which they pafs, where there is an abundance of fifh. There are likewife numerous iflands which are for the moft part cleared up and very pleafant, the moft of them containing great quantities of vines and wild fruits.

With regard to the regions further weft, we cannot well determine their extent, fince the people here have no knowl-**edge** of them except for two or three hundred leagues or **more** wefterly, from whence comes the great river, which paffes, among other places, through a lake having an extent of nearly thirty days' journey by canoe, namely that which we have called the *Mer Douce*. This is of great extent, being nearly four hundred leagues long. Inafmuch as the favages, with whom we are on friendly terms, are at war with other nations on the weft of this great lake, we cannot obtain a more complete knowledge of them, except as they have told us feveral times that fome prifoners from the diftance of **a** hundred leagues had reported that there were tribes there like ourfelves in color and in other refpects.

Through

coaft of the St. Lawrence and the lakes.   north, even to the fouthern borders of
he now refers to the country ftill further   Hudfon's Bay.   *Vide* small map.

Through them they have feen the hair of thefe people, which is very light, and which they efteem highly, faying that it is like our own. I can only conjecture in regard to this, that the people they fay refemble us were thofe more civilized than themfelves. It would require actual prefence to afcertain the truth in regard to this matter. But affiftance is needed, and it is only men of means, leifure, and energy, who could or would undertake **to** promote this enterprife fo that a full exploration of thefe places might be made, affording us a complete knowledge of them.

In regard to the region fouth of the great river it is very thickly fettled, much more fo than that on the north, and by tribes who are at war with each other. The country is very pleafant, much more fo than that on the northern border, and the air is more temperate. There are many kinds of trees and fruits not found north of the river, while there are many things on the north fide, in compenfation, not found on the fouth. The regions towards the eaft are fufficiently well known, inafmuch as the ocean borders thefe places. Thefe are the coafts of Labrador, Newfoundland, Cape Breton, La Cadie, and the Almouchiquois,[187] places well known, as I have treated of them fufficiently in the narrative of my previous voyages, as likewife of the people living there, on which account I fhall not fpeak of them in this treatife, my object being only to make a fuccinct and true report of what I have feen in addition.

The country of the nation of the Attigouantans is in latitude

[187] *Almouchiquois,* fo in the French for Almouchiquois. All the tribes at and fouth of *Choüacoet,* or the mouth of the Saco River, were denominated Almouchiquois by the French. *Vide* Vol II. p. 63, *et paffim.*

tude 44° 30'. and extends two hundred and thirty leagues[188] in length westerly, and ten in breadth. It contains eighteen villages, fix of which are enclofed and fortified by palifades of wood **in** triple rows, bound together, on the top of which **are** galleries, which they provide with ftones and water ; the **former to** hurl upon their enemies and the latter to extinguifh the fire which their enemies may fet to the palifades. The country is pleafant, moft of it cleared up. It has the fhape of Brittany, and is fimilarly fituated, being almoft furrounded by the *Mer Douce*.[189] They affume that thefe eighteen villages are inhabited by two thoufand warriors, not including the common mafs which amounts to perhaps thirty thoufand fouls.

Their cabins are in the fhape of tunnels or arbors, and are covered with the **bark of** trees. They are from twenty-five to thirty fathoms long, more or lefs, and fix wide, having a paffage-way through the middle from ten to twelve feet wide, which extends from one end to the other. On the two fides there is a kind of bench, four feet high, where they fleep in fummer, in order to avoid the annoyance of the fleas, of which there are great numbers. In winter they fleep on the ground on mats near the fire, fo as to be warmer than they would

---

[188] The country of the Attigouantans, fometimes written Attigouautans, the principal tribe of the Hurons, ufed by Champlain as including the whole, with whom the French were in clofe alliance, was from eaft to weft not more than about twelve leagues. There muft have been fome error by which the author is made to fay that it was *two hundred and thirty leagues*. Laverdière fuggefts that in the manufcript it might

have been 23, or 20 to 30, and that the printer made it 230.

[189] The author plainly means that the country of the Hurons was nearly furrounded by the Mer Douce ; that is to fay, by Lake Huron and the waters connected with it, viz, the River Severn, Lake Couchiching, and Lake Simcoe. As to the population, compare *The Jefuits in North America*, by Francis Parkman, LL.D., note p. xxv.

would be on the platform. They lay up a ftock of dry **wood**, with which they fill their cabins, to burn in winter. **At the** extremity of the cabins there is a fpace, where they preferve their Indian corn, which they put into great cafks made of the bark of trees and placed in the middle of their encampment. They have pieces of wood fufpended, on which they put their clothes, provifions, and other things, for fear of the mice, of which there are great numbers. **In one of** thefe cabins there may be twelve fires, and twenty-four families. It fmokes exceffively, from which it follows that **many** receive ferious injury to the eyes, fo that they lofe their fight towards the clofe of life. There is no window nor any opening, except that in the upper part of their cabins for the fmoke to efcape.

This is all that I have been able to learn about their mode of life; and I have defcribed to you fully the kind of dwelling of thefe people, as far as I have been able to learn it, which is the fame as that of all the tribes living in thefe regions. They fometimes change their villages at intervals of ten, twenty, or thirty years, and transfer them to a diftance of one, two, or three leagues from the preceding fituation,[180] except when compelled by their enemies to diflodge, in which cafe they retire to a greater diftance, **as the** Antouhonorons, who went fome forty to fifty leagues. This is the form of their dwellings, which are feparated from each other fome three or four paces, for fear of fire, of which they are in great dread.

Their life is a miferable one in comparifon with our own; but

---

[180] *Vide antea*, note 172, for the reafon of thefe removals.

but they are happy among themfelves, not having experienced anything better, and not imagining that anything
more excellent is to be found. Their principal articles of
food **are** Indian corn and Brazilian beans,[191] which they
prepare in various ways. By braying in a wooden mortar
they reduce the corn to meal. They remove the bran
by means of fans made of the bark of trees. From this
meal they make bread, ufing alfo beans which they firft
boil, as they do the Indian corn for foup, fo that they may
be more eafily crufhed. Then they mix all together, fometimes adding blueberries [192] or dry rafpberries, and fometimes
pieces of deer's fat, though not often, as this is fcarce with
them. After fteeping the whole in lukewarm water, they
make bread in the form of bannocks or pies, which they
bake in the afhes. After they are baked they wafh them,
and from thefe they often make others by wrapping them in
corn leaves, which they faften to them, and then putting them
in boiling water.

But this is not their moft common kind. They make another, which they call *migan*, which is as follows: They
take the pounded Indian corn, without removing the bran,
and put two or three handfuls of it in an earthen pot full of
water. This they boil, ftirring it from time to time, that it
may not burn nor adhere to the pot. Then they put into
the

[191] *Febues du Bréfil.* This was undoubtedly the common trailing bean,
Phafeolus vulgaris, probably called the
Brazilian bean, becaufe it refembled a
bean known under that name. It was
found in cultivation in New England
as mentioned by Champlain and the
early Englifh fettlers. Bradford dif-
couring of the Indians, *His. Plymouth
Plantation,* p. 83, fpeaks of "their
beans of various colfours." It is poffible
that the name, *febues du Bréfil,* was
given to it on account of its red color,
as was that of the Brazil wood, from the
Portuguefe word *braza,* a burning coal.

[192] *Vide antea,* note 101.

the pot a small quantity of fish, fresh or dry, according **to** the season, to give a flavor to the *migan*, as they call it. They make it very often, although it smells badly, especially in winter, either because they do not know how to prepare it rightly, or do not wish to take the trouble to do so. They make two kinds of it, and prepare it very well when they choose. When they use fish the *migan* does not smell badly, but only when it is made with venison. After it is all cooked, they take out the fish, pound **it very fine, and** then put it all together into the pot, not taking **the trouble** to remove the appendages, scales, or inwards, as we do, which generally causes a bad taste. It being thus prepared, they deal out to each one his portion. This *migan* is very thin, and without much substance, as may be well supposed. As for drink, there is no need of it, the *migan* being sufficiently thin of itself.

They have another kind of *migan*, namely, they roast new corn before it is ripe, which they preserve and cook whole with fish, or flesh when they have it. Another way is this: they take Indian corn, which is very dry, roast it in the ashes, then bray it and reduce it to meal as in the former case. This they lay up for the journeys which they undertake here and there. The *migan* made in the latter manner is the best according to my taste. Figure H shows the women braying their Indian corn. In preparing it, they cook a large quantity of fish and meat, which they cut into pieces and put into great kettles, which they fill with water and let it all boil well. When this is done, they gather with a spoon from the surface the fat which comes from the meat and fish. Then they put in the meal of the roasted

corn,

corn, conftantly ftirring it until the *migan* is cooked and
thick as foup. They give to each one a portion, together
with a fpoonful of the fat. This difh they are accuftomed to
prepare for banquets, but they do not generally make it.

Now the corn frefhly roafted, as above defcribed, is highly
efteemed among them. They eat alfo beans, which they boil
with the mafs of the roafted flour, mixing in a little fat and
fifh. Dogs are in requeft at their banquets, which they often
celebrate among themfelves, efpecially in winter, when they
are at leifure. In cafe they go hunting for deer or go fifhing, they lay afide what they get for celebrating thefe banquets, nothing remaining in their cabins but the ufual thin
migan, refembling bran and water, fuch as is given to hogs
to eat.

They have another way of eating the Indian corn. In
preparing it, they take it in the ear and put it in water under
the mud, leaving it two or three months in this ftate until
they think it is putrefied. Then they remove it, and eat it
boiled with meat or fifh. They alfo roaft it, and it is better
fo than boiled. But I affure you that there is nothing that
fmells fo badly as this corn as it comes from the water all
muddy. Yet the women and children take it and fuck it
like fugar-cane, nothing feeming to them to tafte better, as
they fhow by their manner. In general they have two
meals a day. As for ourfelves, we fafted all of Lent and
longer, in order to influence them by our example. But it
was time loft.

They alfo fatten bears, which they keep two or three
years, for the purpofe of their banquets. I obferved that if
this people had domeftic animals they would be interefted
in

in them and care for them very well, and I fhowed them **the** way to keep them, which would be an eafy thing for them, fince they have good grazing grounds in their country, and in large quantities, for all kinds of animals, horfes, oxen, cows, fheep, fwine, and other kinds, for lack of which one would confider them badly off, as they feem to be. Yet with all their drawbacks they feem to me to live happily among themfelves, fince their only ambition **is** to live and fupport themfelves, and they lead a more fettled life than thofe who wander through the forefts like brute beafts. **They** eat many fquafhes,[128] which they boil, and roaft in the afhes.

In regard to their drefs, they have various kinds and ftyles made of the fkins of wild beafts, both thofe which they capture themfelves, and others which they get in exchange for their Indian corn, meal, porcelain, and fifhing-nets from the Algonquins, Nipiffings, and other tribes, which are hunters having no fixed abodes. All their clothes are of one uniform fhape, not varied by any new ftyles. They prepare and fit very well the fkins, making their breeches of deer-fkin rather large, and their ftockings of another piece, which extend up to the middle and have many folds. Their fhoes are made of the fkins of deer, bears, and beaver, of which they ufe great numbers. Befides, they have a robe of the fame fur, in the form of a cloak, which they wear in the Irifh or Egyptian ftyle, with fleeves which are attached with a ftring behind. This is the way they are dreffed in winter, as is feen in figure D. When they go into the fields, they gird up their robe about the body; but when in the village, they

[128] *Sitrouelles*, or *citrouilles*, the common fummer fquafh, *Cucurbita poly-* *morphas.* *Vide* Vol. II. note 128. For figure D, *vide* p. 116.

they leave off their sleeves and do not gird themselves. The Milan trimmings for decorating their garments are made of glue and the scrapings of the before-mentioned skins, of which **they make** bands in various styles according to their **fancy,** putting in places bands of red and brown color amid **those of the** glue, which always keep a whitish appearance, not losing at all their shape, however dirty they may get. There are those among these nations who are much more skilful than others in fitting the skins, and ingenious in inventing ornaments to put on their garments. It is our Montagnais and Algonquins, above all others, who take more pains in this matter. They put on their robes bands of porcupine quills, which they dye a very fine scarlet color.[194] They value these bands very highly, and detach them so that they may serve for other robes when they wish to make **a change.** They also make use of them to adorn the face, **in order** to give it a more graceful appearance whenever they **wish** particularly to decorate themselves.

Most of them paint the face black and red. These colors they mix with oil made from the seed of the sun-flower, or with bear's fat or that of other animals. They also dye their hair, which some wear long, others short, others on one side only. The women and girls always wear their hair in one uniform style. They are dressed like men, except that they always have their robes girt about them, which extend down

to

---

[194] The coloring matter appears to have been derived from the root of the bedstraw, *Galium tinctorium.* Peter Kalm, a pupil of Linnæus, who travelled in Canada in 1749, says, "The roots of this plant are employed by the Indians in dyeing the quills of the American porcupines red, which they put into several pieces of their work, and air, sun, or water seldom change this color." *Travels into North America,* London, 1771, Vol. III, pp. 14-15.

to the knee. They are not at all afhamed to expofe **the** body from the middle up and from the knees down, unlike the men, the reft being always covered. They are loaded with quantities of porcelain, in the fhape of necklaces and chains, which they arrange in the front of their robes and attach to their waifts. They alfo wear bracelets and ear-rings. They have their hair carefully combed, dyed, and oiled. Thus they go to the dance, with a knot **of their hair** behind bound up with eel-fkin, which they ufe as **a cord.** Some-times they put on plates a foot fquare, covered **with** porce-lain, which hang on the back. Thus gaily dreffed and habited, they delight to appear in the dance, to which their fathers and mothers fend them, forgetting nothing that they can devife to embellifh and fet off their daughters. I can teftify that I have feen at dances a girl who had more than twelve pounds of porcelain on her perfon, not including the other bagatelles with which they are loaded and bedecked. **In** the illuftration already cited, F fhows the drefs of the women, G that of the girls attired for the dance.

All thefe people have a very jovial difpofition, although there are many of them who have a fad and gloomy look. Their bodies are well proportioned. Some of the men and women are well formed, ftrong, and robuft. There is a mod-erate number of pleafing and pretty girls, in refpect to figure, color, and expreffion, all being in harmony. Their blood is but little deteriorated, except when they are old. There are among thefe tribes powerful women of extraordinary height. Thefe have almoft the entire care of the houfe and work; namely, they till the land, plant the Indian corn, lay up a ftore of wood for the winter, beat the hemp and fpin it,

making

making from the thread fishing-nets and other useful things. The women harvest the corn, house it, prepare it for eating, and attend **to** household matters. Moreover they are expected to attend their husbands from place to place in the fields, filling the office of pack-mule in carrying the baggage, and to do a thousand other things. All the men do is to hunt for deer and other animals, fish, make their cabins, and go to war. Having done these things, they then go to other tribes with which they are acquainted to traffic and make exchanges. On their return, they give themselves up to festivities and dances, which they give to each other, and when these are over they go to sleep, which they like to do best of all things.

They have some sort of marriage, which is as follows: when a girl has reached the age of eleven, twelve, thirteen, fourteen, or fifteen years she has suitors, more or less according **to** her attractions, who woo her for some time. After **this,** the consent of their fathers and mothers is asked, to whose will the girls often do not submit, although the most discreet and considerate do so. The lover or suitor presents to the girl some necklaces, chains, and bracelets of porcelain. If the girl finds the suitor agreeable, she receives the present. Then the lover comes and remains with her three or four nights, without saying anything to her during the time. They receive thus the fruit of their affections. Whence it happens very often that, after from eight to fifteen days, if they cannot agree, she quits her suitor, who forfeits his necklaces and other presents that he has made, having received in return only a meagre satisfaction. Being thus disappointed in his hopes, the man seeks another woman, and the

girl

girl another fuitor, if it feems to them defirable. Thus they continue to do until a favorable union is formed. It fometimes happens that a girl thus paffes her entire youth, having more than twenty mates, which twenty are not alone in the enjoyment of the creature, mated though they are; for when night comes the young women run from one cabin to another, as do alfo the young men on their part, going where it feems good to them, but always without any violence, referring the whole matter to the pleafure **of the woman.** Their mates will do likewife to their women-neighbors, no jealoufy arifing among them on that account, nor do they incur any reproach or infult, fuch being the cuftom of the country.

Now the time when they do not leave their mates is when they have children. The preceding mate returns to her, renews the affection and friendfhip which he had borne her in the paft, afferting that it is greater than that of any other one, and that the child fhe has is his and of his begetting. The next fays the fame to her. In fine, the victory is with the ftronger, who takes the woman for his wife. Thus it depends upon the choice of the woman to take and accept him who fhall pleafe her beft, having meantime in her fearching and loves gained much porcelain and, befides, the choice of a hufband. The woman remains with him without leaving him; or if fhe do leave him, for he is on trial, it muft be for fome good reafon other than impotence. But while with this hufband, fhe does not ceafe to give herfelf free rein, yet remains always at home, keeping up a good appearance. Thus the children which they have together, born from fuch a woman, cannot be fure of their legitimacy. Accordingly,

in

in view of this uncertainty, it is their custom that the children never succeed to the property and honors of their fathers, there being doubt, as above indicated, as to their **paternity.** They make, however, the children of their sisters, **from** whom they are known to have issued, their successors and heirs.

The following is the way they nourish and bring up their children : they place them during the day on a little wooden board, wrapping them up in furs or skins. To this board they bind them, placing them in an erect position, and leaving a little opening for the child to do its necessities. If it is a girl, they put a leaf of Indian corn between the thighs, which presses against its privates. The extremity of the leaf is carried outside in a turned position, so that the water of the child runs off on it without inconvenience. They put also under the children the down of certain reeds that we call **hare's-foot,** on which they rest very softly. They also clean them with the same down. As an ornament for the child, they adorn the board with beads, which they also put on its neck. however small it may be. At night they put it to bed, entirely naked, between the father and mother. It may be regarded as a great miracle that God should thus preserve it so that no harm befalls it, as might be expected, from suffocation, while the father and mother are in deep sleep, but that rarely happens. The children have great freedom among these tribes. The fathers and mothers indulge them too much, and never punish them. Accordingly they are so bad and of so vicious a nature, that they often strike their mothers and others. The most vicious, when they have acquired the strength and power, strike their fathers. They do this whenever

ever the father or mother does anything that does **not pleafe** them. This is a fort of curfe that God inflicts upon them.

In refpect to laws, I have not been able to find out that they have any, or anything that approaches them, inafmuch as there is not among them any correction, punifhment, or cenfure of evil-doers except in the way of vengeance, when they return evil for evil, not by rule but by paffion, which produces among them conflicts and differences, which occur very frequently.

Moreover, they do not recognize any divinity, or worfhip any God and believe in anything whatever, but live **like** brute beafts. They have, however, fome refpect for the devil, or fomething fo called, which is a matter of uncertainty, fince the word which they ufe thus has various fignifications and comprifes in itfelf various things. It is accordingly difficult to determine whether they mean the devil or fomething elfe, but what efpecially leads to the belief that what they mean is the devil is this: whenever they fee a man doing fomething extraordinary, or who is more capable than ufual, or is a valiant warrior, or furthermore who is in a rage as if out of his reafon and fenfes, they call him *oqui*, or, as we fhould fay, a great knowing fpirit, or a **great** devil. However this may be, they have certain perfons, who are the *oqui*, or, as the Algonquins and Montagnais call them, *manitous*; and perfons of this kind are the medicine-men, who heal the fick, bind up the wounded, and predict future events, who in fine practife all abufes and illufions of the devil to deceive and delude them. Thefe *oquis* or conjurers perfuade their patients and the fick to make, or have made banquets and ceremonies that they may be the fooner
healed.

healed, their object being to participate in them finally themfelves and get the principal benefit therefrom. Under the
pretence of a more fpeedy cure, they likewife caufe them to
obferve various other ceremonies, which I fhall hereafter
fpeak **of in** the proper place. Thefe are the people in whom
they put efpecial confidence, but it is rare that they are poffeffed of the devil and tormented like other favages living
more remote than themfelves.

This gives additional reafon and ground to believe that
their converfion to the knowledge of God would be more
eafy, if their country were inhabited by perfons who would
take the trouble and pains to inftruct them. But it is not
enough to fend to them friars, unlefs there are thofe to fupport and affift them. For although thefe people have the
defire to-day to know what God is, to-morrow this difpofition will change when they are obliged to lay afide and bring
under their foul ways, their diffolute manners, and their
favage indulgences. So that there is need of people and
families to keep them in the way of duty, to conftrain them
through mildnefs to do better, and to move them by good
example to mend their lives. Father Jofeph [106] and myfelf
have many times conferred with them in regard to our
belief, laws, and cuftoms. They liftened attentively in their
affemblies, fometimes faying to us : You fay things that pafs
our knowledge, and which we cannot underfland by words,
being beyond our comprehenfion ; but if you would do us a
fervice come and dwell in this country, bringing your wives
and children, and when they are here we fhall fee how you
                                                         ferve

---

[106] Père Jofeph Le Caron, who had paffed the winter among the Hurons.

ferve the God you worſhip, and how you live with your
wives and children, how you cultivate and plant the **foil**,
how you obey your laws, how you take care of animals,
and how you manufacture all that we ſee proceeding from
your inventive ſkill. When we ſee all this, we ſhall learn
more in a year than in twenty by ſimply hearing you diſ-
courſe; and if we cannot then underſtand, you ſhall take
our children, who ſhall be as your own. And thus being
convinced that our life is a miſerable one **in compariſon**
with yours, it is eaſy to believe that we ſhall adopt yours,
abandoning our own.

Their words ſeemed to me good common ſenſe, ſhowing
the deſire they have to get a knowledge of God. It is a
great wrong to let ſo many men be loſt, and ſee them periſh
at our door, without rendering them the ſuccor which can
only be given through the help of kings, princes, and eccle-
ſiaſtics, who alone have the power to do this. For to them
alone belongs the honor of ſo great a work; namely, planting
the Chriſtian faith in an unknown region and among ſavage
nations, ſince we are well informed about theſe people, that
they long for and deſire nothing ſo much as to be clearly
inſtructed as to what they ſhould do and avoid. It is accordingly the duty of thoſe who have the power, to labor
there and contribute of their abundance, for one day they
muſt anſwer before God for the loſs of the ſouls which they
allowed to periſh through their negligence and avarice; and
theſe are not few but very numerous. Now this will be
done when it ſhall pleaſe God to give them grace to this
end. As for myſelf, I deſire this reſult rather to-day than
to-morrow, from the zeal which I have for the advancement
of

of God's glory, for the honor of my King, and for the welfare and renown of my country.

When **they are** fick, the man or woman who is attacked **with any difeafe fends** for the *oqui*, who vifits the patient **and informs** himfelf about the malady and the fuffering. After this, **the** *oqui* fends for a large number of men, women, and girls, including three or four old women. Thefe enter the cabin of the fick, dancing, each one having on his head the fkin of a bear or fome other wild beaft, that of the bear being the moft common as it is the moft frightful. There are three or four other old women about the fick or fuffering, who for the moft part feign ficknefs, or are fick merely in imagination. But they are foon cured of this ficknefs, and generally make banquets at the expenfe of their friends or relatives, **who give** them fomething to put into their kettle, **in** addition **to the** prefents which they receive from **the dancers, fuch** as porcelain and other bagatelles, fo that they **are** foon cured; **for** when they find that they have nothing more to look for, they get up with what they have fecured. But thofe who are really fick are not readily cured by plays, dances, and fuch proceedings.

To return to my narrative: the old women near the fick perfon receive the prefents, each finging and paufing in turn. When all the prefents have been made, they proceed to lift up their voices with one accord, all finging together and keeping time with fticks on pieces of dry bark. Then all the women and girls proceed to the end of the cabin, as if they were about to begin a ballet or mafquerade. The old women walk in front with their bearfkins on their heads, all the others following them, one after the other. They have only two

                                                                kinds

kinds of dances with regular time, one of four steps and **the** other of twelve, as in the *trioli* de Bretagne. They exhibit much grace in dancing. Young men often take part with them. After dancing an hour or two, the old women lead out the fick perfon to dance, who gets up dolefully and prepares to dance, and after a fhort time fhe dances and enjoys as much as the others. I leave it to you to confider how fick fhe was. Below is reprefented the mode of their dances.

The medicine-man thus gains honor and credit, his patient being fo foon healed and on her feet. This treatment, however, does nothing for thofe who are dangeroufly ill and reduced by weaknefs, but caufes their death rather than their cure; for I can teftify that they fometimes make fuch a noife and hubbub from morning until two o'clock at night that it is impoffible for the patient to endure it without great pain. Sometimes the patient is feized with the defire to have the women and girls dance all together, which is done in accordance with the direction of the *ogui*. But this is not all, for he and the *manitou*, accompanied by fome others, make grimaces, perform magic arts, and twift themfelves about fo that they generally end in being out of their fenfes, feemingly crazy, throwing the fire from one fide of the cabin to the other, eating burning coals, holding them in their hands for a while, and throwing red-hot afhes into the eyes of the fpectators. Seeing them in this condition, one would fay that the devil, the *ogui*, or *manitou*, if he is thus to be called, poffeffes and torments them. This noife and hubbub being over, they retire each to his own cabin.

But thofe who fuffer efpecially during this time are the

wives

wives of thofe poffeffed, and all the inmates of their cabins, from the fear they have left the raging ones burn up all that is in their houfes. This leads them to remove everything that **is** in fight; for as foon as he arrives he is all in a **fury**, his eyes flafhing and frightful, fometimes ftanding up, fometimes feated, as his fancy takes him. Suddenly a fit feizes him, and laying hold of everything he finds in his way he throws them to one fide and the other. Then he lies down and fleeps for fome time. Waking up with a jump, he feizes fire and ftones which he throws about reck-lefsly on all fides. This rage paffes off with the fleep which feizes him again. Then he rages and calls feveral of his friends to fweat with him. The latter is the beft means they have for preferving themfelves in health. While they are fweating, **the** kettle boils to prepare them fomething to eat. They **remain,** two or three hours or fo, covered up with great **pieces** of bark and wrapped in their robes, with a great many ftones about them which have been heated red hot in the fire. They fing all the time while they are in the rage, occa-fionally ftopping to take breath. Then they give them many draughts of water to drink, fince they are very thirfty, when the demoniac, who was crazy or poffeffed of an evil fpirit, becomes fober.

Thus it happens that three or four of thefe fick perfons get well, rather by a happy coincidence and chance than in confequence of any intelligent treatment, and this con-firms their falfe belief that they are healed by means of thefe ceremonies, not confidering that, for two who are thus cured, ten others die on account of the noife, great hubbub and hiffing, which are rather calculated to kill than cure

a

a fick perfon. But that they expect to recover their **health**
by this noife, and we on the contrary by filence and reft,
fhows how the devil does everything in hoftility to the good.

There are alfo women who go into thefe rages, but they
do not do fo much harm. They walk on all fours like beafts.
Seeing this, the magician, called *oqui*, begins to fing; then,
with fome contortions of the face, he blows **upon** her, directing her to drink certain waters, and make **at once a** banquet
of fifh or flefh, which muft be procured although **very fcarce**
at the time. When the fhouting is over and the **banquet**
ended, they return each to her own cabin. At another time
he comes back and vifits her, blowing upon her and finging
in company with feveral others, who have been fummoned
for this purpofe, and who hold in the hand a dry tortoife-fhell
filled with little pebbles, which they caufe to refound in the
ears of the fick woman. They direct her to make at once
three or four banquets with finging and dancing, when all
the girls appear adorned and painted as I have reprefented
in figure G. The *oqui* orders mafquerades, and directs
them to difguife themfelves, as thofe do who run along the
ftreets in France on *Mardi-gras*.[306] Thus they go and fing
near the bed of the fick woman and promenade through the
village while the banquet is preparing to receive the mafkers,
who return very tired, having taken exercife enough to be
able to empty the kettle of its *migan*.

According to their cuftom each houfehold lives on what
it gets by fifhing and planting, improving as much land as it
needs. They clear it up with great difficulty, fince they do
not

---

[306] *Mardi-gras*, Shrove-Tuefday, or nival, the day before Afh Wednefday,
flefh Tuefday, the laft day of the Car- the firft day in Lent.

not have the implements adapted to this purpose. A party strip the trees of all their branches, which they burn at their base in **order** to kill them. They clear carefully the **land between the** trees, and then plant their corn at distances of a pace, putting in each place some ten kernels, and **so on until** they have made provision for three or four years, fearing that a bad year may befall them. The women attend to the planting and harvesting, as I have said before, and to procuring a supply of wood for winter. All the women aid each other in procuring this provision of wood, which they do in the month of March or April, in the order of two days for each. Every household is provided with as much as it needs; and if a girl marries, each woman and girl is expected to carry to the newly married one a parcel of wood for her provision, since she could not procure it alone, and **at a** season when she has to give her attention to other **things**.

The following is their mode of government: the older **and** leading men assemble in a council, in which they settle upon and propose all that is necessary for the affairs of the village. This is done by a plurality of voices, or in accordance with the advice of some one among them whose judgment they consider superior: such a one is requested by the company to give his opinion on the propositions that have been made, and this opinion is minutely obeyed. They have no particular chiefs with absolute command, but they show honor to the older and more courageous men, whom they **name** captains, as a mark of honor and respect, of which there are several in a village. But, although they confer more honor upon one than upon others, yet he is not

on

on that account to bear fway, nor efteem himfelf higher
than his companions, unlefs he does fo from vanity. They
make no ufe of punifhments nor arbitrary command, but
accomplifh everything by the entreaties of the feniors, and
by means of addreffes and remonftrances. Thus and not
otherwife do they bring everything to pafs.

They all deliberate in common, and whenever any member of the affembly offers to do anything for the welfare of the
village, or to go anywhere for the fervice of **the community,**
he is requefted to prefent himfelf, and if he is **judged capa-**
ble of carrying out what he propofes, they exhort him, **by fair**
and favorable words, to do his duty. They declare him to be
an energetic man, fit for undertakings, and affure him that
he will win honor in accomplifhing them. In a word, they
encourage him by flatteries, in order that this favorable difpofition of his for the welfare of his fellow-citizens may
continue and increafe. Then, according to his pleafure, he
refufes the refponfibility, which few do, or accepts, fince
thereby he is held in high efteem.

When they engage in wars or go to the country of their
enemies, two or three of the older or valiant captains make
a beginning in the matter, and proceed to the adjoining
villages to communicate their purpofe, and make prefents to
the people of thefe villages, in order to induce them to
accompany them to the wars in queftion. In fo far they act
as generals of armies. They defignate the place where they
defire to go, difpofe of the prifoners who are captured, and
have the direction of other matters of efpecial importance,
of which they get the honor, if they are fuccefsful; but, if
not, the difgrace of failure in the war falls upon them.
Thefe

Thefe captains alone are looked upon and confidered as chiefs of the tribes.

They have, moreover, general affemblies, with reprefenta-tives from remote regions. Thefe reprefentatives come every **year, one from** each province, and meet in a town defignated as the rendezvous of the affembly. Here are celebrated great banquets and dances, for three weeks or a month, according as they may determine. Here they renew their friendfhip, refolve upon and decree what they think beft for the prefer-vation of their country againft their enemies, and make each other handfome prefents, after which they retire each to his own diftrict.

In burying the dead, they take the body of the deceafed, wrap it in **furs,** and cover it very carefully with the bark of trees. **Then they** place it in a cabin, of the length of the body, **made of bark** and erected upon four pofts. Others **they place in the** ground, propping up the earth on all **fides,** that **it** may not fall on the body, which they cover **with** the bark of trees, putting earth on top. Over this trench they alfo make a little cabin. Now it is to be under-ftood that the bodies remain in thefe places, thus inhumed, but for a period of eight or ten years, when the men of the village recommend the place where their ceremonies are to take place; or, to fpeak more precifely, they hold a general council, in which all the people of the country are prefent, for the purpofe of defignating the place where a feftival is to be held. After this they return each to his own **village, where** they take all the bones of the deceafed, ftrip them and make them quite clean. Thefe they keep very carefully, although they fmell like bodies recently in-terred.

terred. Then all the relatives and friends of the deceafed
take thefe bones, together with their necklaces, furs, axes,
kettles, and other things highly valued, and carry them,
with a quantity of edibles, to the place affigned. Here,
when all have affembled, they put the edibles in a place
defignated by the men of the village, and engage in banquets and continual dancing. The feftival continues for
the fpace of ten days, during which **time other** tribes, from
all quarters, come to witnefs it and the ceremonies. **The**
latter are attended with great outlays.

Now, by means of these ceremonies, including dances,
banquets, and affemblies, as above ftated, they renew their
friendfhip to one another, faying that the bones of their relatives and friends are to be all put together, thus indicating
by a figure that, as their bones are gathered together and
united in one and the fame place, fo ought they alfo, during
their life, to be united in one friendfhip and harmony, like
relatives and friends, without feparation. Having thus min-
gled together the bones of their mutual relatives and friends,
they pronounce many difcourfes on the occafion. Then, after
various grimaces or exhibitions, they make a great trench, ten
fathoms fquare, in which they put the bones, together with
the necklaces, chains of porcelain, axes, kettles, fword-blades,
knives, and various other trifles, which, however, are of no
flight account in their eftimation. They cover the whole
with earth, putting on top feveral great pieces of wood, and
placing around many pofts, on which they put a covering.
This is their manner of proceeding with regard to the dead,
and it is the moft prominent ceremony they have. Some
of them believe in the immortality of the foul, while others
have

have only a prefentiment of it, which, however, is not fo
very different; for they fay that after their deceafe they will
go to **a place** where they will fing, like crows, a fong, it muft
be **confeffed,** quite different from that of angels. On the
following **page** are reprefented their fepulchres and manner
of interment.

It remains to defcribe how they fpend their time in winter; namely, from the month of December to the end of
March, or the beginning of our fpring, when the fnow
melts. All that they might do during autumn, as I have
before ftated, they poftpone to be done during winter;
namely, their banquetings, and ufual dances for the fake of
the fick, which I have already defcribed, and the affemblages
of the inhabitants of various villages, where there are banquetings, finging, and dances, which they call *tabagies*,[187] and
where fometimes five hundred perfons are collected, both
men, women, and girls. The latter are finely decked and
adorned with the beft and moft coftly things they have.

On certain days they make mafquerades, and vifit each
other's cabins, afking for the things they like, and if they
meet thofe who have what they want, these give it to them
freely. Thus they go on afking for many things without
end; fo that a fingle one of thofe foliciting will have robes
of beaver, bear, deer, lynxes, and other furs, alfo fifh, Indian
corn, tobacco, or boilers kettles, pots, axes, pruning-knives,
knives, and other like things. They go to the houfes and
cabins of the village, finging thefe words, That one gave
me this, another gave that, or like words, by way of com-
mendation

187 *Vide* Vol. I, pp. 236-238.

mendation. But if one gives them nothing they get angry,
and fhow fuch fpite towards him that when they leave they
take a ftone and put it near this man or that woman who
has not given them anything. Then, without faying a
word, they return finging, which is a mark of infult, cenfure,
and ill-will. The women do fo as well as the men, and this
mode of proceeding takes place at night, and the mafquerade continues feven or eight days. There **are fome of** their
villages which have mafkers or merry-makers, as **we do on**
the evening of *Mardi-gras*, and they invite the **other vil-**
lages to come and fee them and win their utenfils, if **they**
can. Meanwhile banquets are not wanting. This is the
way they fpend their time in winter.

Moreover the women fpin, and pound meal for the journeys
of their hufbands in fummer, who go to other tribes to trade,
as they decide to do at the above-mentioned councils, in
which it is determined what number of men may go from
each village, that it may not be deprived of men of war for
its protection; and nobody goes from the country without
the general confent of the chiefs, or if they fhould go they
would be regarded as behaving improperly. The men make
nets for fifhing, which they carry on in fummer, but generally in winter, when they capture the fifh under the ice with
the line or with the feine.

The following is their manner of fifhing. They make
feveral holes in a circular form in the ice, the one where
they are to draw the feine being fome five feet long and
three wide. Then they proceed to place their net at this
opening, attaching it to a rod of wood from fix to feven feet
long, which they put under the ice. This rod they caufe to
pafs

pass from hole to hole, when one or more men, putting their hands in the holes, take hold of the rod to which is attached an end of the net, until they unite at the opening of five to six **feet.** Then they let the net drop to the bottom of the **water, it** being sunk by little stones attached to the end. **After it** is down they draw it up again with their arms at its two ends, thus capturing the fish that are in it. This is, in brief, their manner of fishing in winter.

The winter begins in the month of November and continues until the month of April, when the trees begin to send forth the sap and show their buds.

On the 22d of the month of April we received news from our interpreter, who had gone to Carantoüan, through those who had come from there. They told us that they had left him on the road, he having returned to the village for certain reasons.

Now, resuming the thread of my narrative, our savages assembled to come with us, and conduct us back to our habitation, and for this purpose we set out from their country on the 20th of the month,[104] and were forty days on the way. We caught a large number of fish and animals of various kinds, together with small game, which afforded us especial pleasure, in addition to the provisions thus furnished us for our journey. Upon our arrival among the French, towards the end of the month of June, I found Sieur du Pont Gravé, who had come from France with two vessels, and who had almost despaired of seeing me again, having heard from the savages the bad news, that I was dead.

We

---

[104] This must have been on the 20th of May.

We alſo ſaw all the holy fathers who had remained at our ſettlement. They too were very happy to ſee us again, and we none the leſs ſo to ſee them. Welcomes and felicitations on all ſides being over, I made arrangements to ſet out from the Falls of St. Louis for our ſettlement, taking with me my hoſt D'Arontal. I took leave alſo of all the other ſavages, aſſuring them of my affection, and that, if I could, I would ſee them in the future, **to aſſiſt them** as I had already done in the paſt, bringing them **valuable preſents** to ſecure their friendſhip with one another, **and begging** them to forget all the diſputes which **they had had** when I reconciled them, which they promiſed to do.

Then we ſet out, on the 8th of July, and arrived at our ſettlement on the 11th of that month. Here I found everybody in good health, and we all, in company with our holy fathers, who chanted the Divine ſervice, returned thanks to God for His care in preſerving us, and protecting us amid the many perils and dangers to which we had been expoſed.

After this, and when everything had become ſettled, I proceeded to ſhow hoſpitalities to my hoſt, D'Arontal, who admired our building, our conduct, and mode of living. After carefully obſerving us, he ſaid to me, in private, that he ſhould never die contented until he had ſeen all of his friends, or at leaſt a good part of them, come and take up their abode with us, in order to learn how to ſerve God, and our way of living, which he eſteemed ſupremely happy in compariſon with their own. Moreover he ſaid that, if he could not learn it by word of mouth, he would do ſo much better and more eaſily by ſight and by frequent intercourſe, and that, if their minds could not comprehend our arts,

ſciences,

sciences, and trades, their children who were young could
do so, as they had often represented to us in their country in
conversation with Father Joseph. He urged us, for the promotion of this object, to make another settlement at the
Falls of St. Louis, so as to secure them the passage of the
river against their enemies, assuring us that, as soon as we
should build a house, they would come in numbers to live
as brothers with us. Accordingly I promised to make a
settlement for them as soon as possible.

After we had remained four or five days together, I
gave him some valuable presents, with which he was greatly
pleased, and I begged him to continue his affection for us,
and come again to see our settlement with his friends.
Then he returned happy to the Falls of St. Louis, where
his companions awaited him.

When this Captain D'Arontal had departed, we enlarged
our habitation by a third at least in buildings and fortifications, since it was not sufficiently spacious, nor convenient
for receiving the members of our own company and likewise
the strangers that might come to see us. We used, in building, lime and sand entirely, which we found very good
there in a spot near the habitation. This is a very useful
material for building for those disposed to adapt and accus-
tom themselves to it.

The Fathers Denis and Joseph determined to return to
France, in order to testify there to all they had seen, and to
the hope they could promise themselves of the conversion of
these people, who awaited only the assistance of the holy
fathers in order to be converted and brought to our faith
and the Catholic religion.

During

During my ftay at the fettlement I had fome common grain cut; namely, French grain, which had been planted there and which had come up very finely, that I might take it to France, as evidence that the land is good and fertile. In another part, moreover, there was fome fine Indian corn, alfo fcions and trees which had been given us by Sieur du Monts in Normandy. In a word, all the gardens of the place were in an admirably **fine** condition, being planted with peas, beans, and other vegetables, **alfo fquafhes** and very fuperior radifhes of various forts, **cabbages, beets,** and other kitchen vegetables. When on the point **of** departure, we left two of our fathers at the fettlement; namely, Fathers Jean d'Olbeau and Pacifique,[199] who were greatly pleafed with all the time fpent at that place, and refolved **to** await there the return of Father Jofeph,[200] who **was** expected to come back in the following year, which he did.

We failed in our barques the 20th day of July, and arrived at Tadouffac the 23d day of the month, where Sieur du Pont Gravé awaited us with his veffel ready and equipped. In this we embarked and fet out the 3d day of the month of Auguft. The wind was fo favorable that we arrived in health by the grace of God, at Honfleur, on the 10th day of September, one thoufand fix hundred and fixteen, and **upon** our arrival rendered praife and thanks to God for his great care in preferving our lives, and delivering and even fnatching us, as it were, from the many dangers to which we had been expofed, and for bringing and conducting us in health

to

[199] Jean d'Olbeau and the lay brother Pacifique du Pleffis.

[200] Jofeph le Caron, who accompanied Champlain to France.

to our country ; we befought Him alfo to move the heart of our King, and the gentlemen of his council, to contribute their affiftance fo far as neceffary to bring thefe poor favages to the knowledge of God, whence honor will redound to his Majefty, grandeur and growth to his realm, profit to his fubjeéts, and the glory of all thefe undertakings and toils to God, the fole author of all excellence, to whom be honor and glory.   Amen.

CONTINUATION OF THE VOYAGES

AND DISCOVERIES MADE IN NEW FRANCE,

BY

SIEUR DE CHAMPLAIN,

CAPTAIN FOR THE KING IN THE WESTERN MARINE,

IN THE YEAR 1618.

———

T the beginning of the year one thoufand fix hundred and eighteen, on the twenty-fecond of March, I fet out from Paris,[201] together with my brother-in-law,[202] for Honfleur, our ufual port of embarkation. There we were obliged to make a long ftay on account of contrary winds. But when they had become favorable, we embarked on the large veffel of the affociation, which Sieur du Pont Gravé commanded. There was alfo on board a nobleman, named De la Mothe,

[201] Champlain made a voyage to New France in 1617, but appears to have kept no journal of its events. He fimply obferves that nothing occurred worthy of remark. *Vide* iffue of 1632, Quebec ed., p. 969. Sagard gives a brief narrative of the events that occurred that year. Vol. I. pp. 34–44.

[202] Euftache Boullé. His father was Nicolas Boullé, Secretary of the King's Chamber, and his mother was Marguerite Alix. *Vide* Vol. I. p. 205 *et paffim*.

la Mothe,[293] who had previously made a voyage with the Jesuits to the regions of La Cadie, where he was taken prisoner by the English, **and** by them carried to the Virginias, the place of their settlement. Some time after they transferred **him** to England and from there to France, where there arose **in** him an increased desire to make another voyage to New France, which led him to seek the opportunity presented by me. I had assured him, accordingly, that I would use my influence and assistance with our associates, as it seemed to me that they would find such a person desirable, since he would be very useful in those regions.

Our embarkation being made, we took our departure from Honfleur on the 24th day of May following, in the year 1618. **The** wind was favorable for our voyage, but continued so only a very few days, when it suddenly changed, and we had all the time head winds up to our arrival, on the 3d day of June following, on the Grand Bank, where the fresh fishery is carried on. Here we perceived to the windward of us some banks of ice, which came down from the north. While waiting for a favorable wind we engaged in fishing, which afforded us great pleasure, not only on account of the fish but also of a kind of bird called *fauquets*,[294] and other kinds that are caught on the line like fish. For, on

---

[293] Nicolas de La Mothe, or de la Motte le Vilin. He had been Lieutenant of Saussaye in 1613 when Capt. Argall captured the French colony at Mount Desert. *Vide Les Voyages de Champlain*, 1632, Quebec ed., p. 773: *Relation de la Nouvelle France*, Père Biard, p. 65.

[294] *Fauquets*. Probably the common Tern, or Sea Swallow *Sterna hirundo*.

Peter Kalm, on his voyage in 1749, says "Terns, *Sterna hirundo*, Linn., though of a somewhat darker colour than the common ones, we found after the forty-first degree of north latitude and forty-seventh degree of west longitude from London, very plentifully, and sometimes in flocks of some hundreds; sometimes they settled, as if tired, on our ship." *Kalm's Travels*, 1770, Vol. I. p. 23.

on throwing the line, with its hook baited with cod liver,
thefe birds made for it with a rufh, and in fuch numbers
that you could not draw it out in order to throw it again,
without capturing them by the beak, feet, and wings as they
flew and fell upon the bait, fo great were the eagernefs and
voracity of thefe birds. This fifhing afforded us great pleafure, not only on account of the fport, but on account of the
infinite number of birds and fifh **that we** captured, which
were very good eating, and made a very defirable change
on fhipboard.

Continuing on our route, we arrived on the 15th **of the**
month off Ifle Percée, and on St. John's day[205] following
entered the harbor of Tadouffac, where we found our fmall
veffel, which had arrived three weeks before us. The men
on her told us that Sieur des Chefnes, the commander, had
gone to our fettlement at Quebec. Thence he was to go to
the Trois Rivières to meet the favages, who were to come
there from various regions for the purpofe of trade, and
likewife to determine what was to be done on account of
the death of two of our men, who had been treacheroufly
and perfidioufly killed by two vicious young men of the
Montagnais. Thefe two unfortunate victims, as the men
on the veffel informed us, had been killed while out hunting
nearly two years[206] before. Thofe in the fettlement had
always fuppofed that they had been drowned from the up-
fetting of their canoe, until a fhort time before, one of the
men, conceiving an animofity againft the murderers, made a
difclofure

---

[205] St. John's day was June 24th.
[206] According to Sagard they were
assassinated about the middle of April,
1617. *Hift. Canada,* Vol. I. p. 42.

difclofure and communicated the fact and caufe of the murder to the men of our fettlement. For certain reafons it has
feemed to me well to give an account of the matter and of
what was done in regard to it. But it is almoft impoffible
to obtain the exact truth in the cafe, on account, not only
of the fmall amount of teftimony at hand, but of the diver-
fity of the ftatements made, the moft of which were pre-
fumptive. I will, however, give an account of the matter
here, following the ftatement of the greater number as being
nearer the truth, and relating what I have found to be the
moft probable.

The following is the occafion of the murder of the two unfortunate deceafed. One of the two murderers paid frequent
vifits to our fettlement, receiving there a thoufand kindneffes
and favors, among other perfons from Sieur du Parc, a nobleman from Normandy, in command at the time at Quebec, in
the fervice of the King and in behalf of the merchants of
the Affociation in the year 1616. This favage, while on one
of his cuftomary vifits, received one day, on account of fome
jealoufy, ill treatment from one of the two murdered men,
who was by profeffion a lockfmith, and who after fome
words beat the favage fo foundly as to imprefs it well upon
his memory. And not fatisfied with beating and mifufing
the favage he incited his companions to do the fame, which
aroufed ftill more the hatred and animofity of the favage
towards this lockfmith and his companions, and led him to
feek an opportunity to revenge himfelf. He accordingly
watched for a time and opportunity for doing fo, acting
however cautioufly and appearing as ufual, without fhowing
any fign of refentment.

Some

Some time after, the lockſmith and a ſailor named Charles
Pillet, from the iſland of Ré, arranged to go hunting **and**
ſtay away three or four nights. For this purpoſe they got
ready a canoe, and embarking departed from Quebec for
Cape Tourmente. Here there were ſome little iſlands
where a great quantity of game and birds reſorted, near
Iſle d'Orleans, and diſtant ſeven leagues from Quebec. The
departure of our men became at once known **to** the two
ſavages, who were not ſlow in ſtarting to purſue them **and**
carry out their evil deſign. They ſought **for the place**
where the lockſmith and his companion went to ſleep, in
order to ſurpriſe them. Having aſcertained it at evening,
at break of day on the following morning, the two ſavages
ſlipped quietly along certain very pleaſant meadows. Arriving at a point near the place in queſtion, they moored their
canoe, landed and went ſtraight to the cabin, where our men
had ſlept. But they found only the lockſmith, who was preparing to go hunting with his companion, and who thought
of nothing leſs than of what was to befall him. One of
theſe ſavages approached him, and with ſome pleaſant words
removed from him all ſuſpicion of anything wrong in order
that he might the better deceive him. But as he ſaw him
ſtoop to adjuſt his arquebus, he quickly drew a club that he
had concealed on his perſon, and gave the lockſmith ſo
heavy a blow on his head, that it ſent him ſtaggering and
completely ſtunned. The ſavage, ſeeing that the lockſmith
was preparing to defend himſelf, repeated his blow, ſtruck
him to the ground, threw himſelf upon him, and with a knife
gave him three or four cuts in the ſtomach, killing him in
this horrible manner.

In

25

In order that they might alfo get poffeffion of the failor, the companion of the lockfmith who had ftarted early in the morning to go hunting, not becaufe they bore any fpecial hatred towards him, but that they might not be difcovered **nor accufed** by him, they went in all directions fearching for **him.** At laft, from the report of an arquebus which they heard, they difcovered where he was, in which direction they rapidly haftened, fo as to give no time to the failor to reload his arquebus and put himfelf in a ftate of defence. Approaching, they fired their arrows at him, by which having proftrated him, they ran upon him and finifhed him with the knife.

Then the affaffins carried off the body, together with the other, and, binding them fo firmly together that they would not come apart, attached to them a quantity of ftones and pebbles, together with their weapons and clothes, fo as not to be difcovered by any fign, after which they carried them **to the middle of** the river, threw them in, and they fank to the bottom. Here they remained a long time until, through the will of God, the cords broke, and the bodies were wafhed afhore and thrown far up on the bank, to ferve as accufers and inconteftable witneffes of the attack of thefe two cruel and treacherous affaffins. For the two bodies were found at a diftance of more than twenty feet from the water in the woods, but had not become feparated in fo long a time, being ftill firmly bound, the bones, ftripped of the flefh like a fkeleton, alone remaining. For the two victims, contrary to the expectation of the two murderers, who thought they **had** done their work fo fecretly that it would never be known, were found a long time after their difappearance by the men of

our

our fettlement, who, pained at their abfence, fearched for them along the banks of the river. But God in his juftice would not permit fo enormous a crime, and had caufed it to be expofed by another favage, their companion, in retaliation for an injury he had received from them. Thus their wicked acts were difclofed.

The holy Fathers and the men of the fettlement were greatly furprifed at feeing the bodies of thefe two unfortunates, with their bones all bare, and their fkulls broken by the blows received from the club of the favages. The Fathers and others at the fettlement advifed to preferve them in fome portion of the fettlement until the return of our veffels, in order to confult with all the French as to the beft courfe to purfue in the matter. Meanwhile our people at the fettlement refolved to be on their guard, and no longer allow fo much freedom to thefe favages as they had been accuftomed to, but on the contrary require reparation for fo cruel a murder by a procefs of juftice, or fome other way, or let things in the mean time remain as they were, in order the better to await our veffels and our return, that we might all together confult what was to be done in the matter.

But the favages feeing that this iniquity was difcovered, and that they and the murderer were obnoxious to the French, were feized with defpair, and, fearing that our men would exercife vengeance upon them for this murder, withdrew for a while from our fettlement.²⁰⁷ Not only thofe guilty of

---

²⁰⁷ Sagard fays the French, on account of this affair, were menaced by eight hundred favages of different nations who were affembled at Trois Rivières. *Vide Hiftoire du Canada*, 1636, Vol. I. p. 42. The ftatement, "on eftoit menacé de

of the act but the others also being seized with fear came no longer to the settlement, as they had been accustomed to do, but waited for greater security for themselves.

Finding themselves deprived of intercourse with us, and of their usual welcome, the savages sent one of their companions named by the French, *La Ferrière*, to make their excuses for this murder; namely, they asserted they had never been accomplices in it, and had never consented to it, and that, if it was desired to have the two murderers for the sake of inflicting justice, the other savages would willingly consent to it, unless the French should be pleased to take as reparation and restitution for the dead some valuable presents of skins, as they are accustomed to do in return for a thing that cannot be restored. They earnestly entreated the French to accept this rather than require the death of the accused which they anticipated would be hard for them to execute, and so doing to forget everything as if it had not occurred.

To this, in accordance with the advice of the holy Fathers, it was decided to reply that the savages should bring and deliver up the two malefactors, in order to ascertain from them their accomplices, and who had incited them to do the deed. This they communicated to La Ferrière for him to report to his companions.

This

de huict cens Sauuages de diuerse nations, qui s'estoient assemblez és Trois Rivieres à dessein de venir surprendre les François & leur coupper à tous la gorge pour preuenir la vengeance qu'ils eussent pû prendre de deux de leurs hommes tuez par les Montagnais enuiron la my Auril de l'an 1617," is, we think, too strong. The savages were excited and frightened by the demands of the French, who desired to produce upon their minds a strong moral impression, in order to prevent a recurrence of the murder, which was a private thing, in which the great body of the savages had no part. They could not be said to be hostile, though they prudently put themselves in a state of defence, as, under the circumstances, it was very natural they should do.

This decision having been made, La Ferrière withdrew **to** his companions, who upon hearing the decision of **the** French found this procedure and mode of justice very strange and difficult; since they have no established law among themselves, but only vengeance and restitution by presents. After considering the whole matter and deliberating with one another upon it, they summoned the two murderers and set forth to them the unhappy position into which they had been thrown by the event of this murder, which might cause a perpetual war with the French, from which their women and children would suffer. However much trouble they might give us, and although they might keep us shut up in our settlement and prevent us from hunting, cultivating and tilling the soil, and although we were in too small numbers to keep the river blockaded, as they persuaded themselves to believe in their consultations; still, after all their deliberations, they concluded that it was better to live in peace with the French than in war and perpetual distrust.

Accordingly the savages thus assembled, after finishing their consultation and representing the situation to the accused, asked them if they would not have the courage to go with them to the settlement of the French and appear before them; promising them that they should receive no harm, and assuring them that the French were lenient and disposed to pardon, and would in short go so far in dealing with them as to overlook their offence on condition of their not returning to such evil ways.

The two criminals, finding themselves convicted in conscience, yielded to this proposition and agreed to follow this advice.

advice. Accordingly one of them made preparations, arraying himfelf in fuch garments and decorations as he could procure, **as** if he had been invited to go to a marriage or fome **great** feftivity. Thus attired, he went to the fettle-**ment,** accompanied by his father, fome of the principal **chiefs,** and the captain of their company. As to the other murderer, he excufed himfelf from this journey,[298] realizing his guilt of the heinous act and fearing punifhment.

When now they had entered the habitation, which was forthwith furrounded by a multitude of the favages of their company, the bridge[299] was drawn up, and all of the French put themfelves on guard, arms in hand. They kept a ftrict watch, fentinels being pofted at the neceffary points, for fear of what the favages outfide might do, fince they fufpected that it was intended actually to inflict punifhment upon the guilty **one,** who had fo freely offered himfelf to our mercy, and not upon him alone, but upon thofe alfo who had accompanied him infide, who likewife were not too fure of their perfons, and who, feeing matters in this ftate, did not expect to get out with their lives. The whole matter was very well managed and carried out, fo as to make them realize the magnitude of the crime and have fear for the future. Otherwife there would have been no fecurity with them, and we fhould have been obliged to live with arms in hand and in perpetual diftruft.

After this, the favages fufpecting left fomething might happen contrary to what they hoped from us, the holy Fathers

---

[298] They were then at Trois Rivières.

[299] The moat around the habitation at Quebec was fifteen feet wide and fix feet deep, conftructed with a drawbridge, to be taken up in cafe of need. *Vide* Vol. II. p 182.

Fathers proceeded to make them an addrefs on the fubject of this crime. They fet forth to them the friendfhip which the French had fhown them for ten or twelve years back, when we began to know them, during which time we had continually lived in peace and intimacy with them, nay even with fuch freedom as could hardly be expreffed. They added moreover that I had in perfon affifted them feveral times in war againft their enemies, thereby **expofing my** life for their welfare; while we were not under **any obligations** to do fo, being impelled only by friendfhip and good **will** towards them, and feeling pity at the miferies and perfecutions which their enemies caufed them to endure and fuffer. This is why we were unable to believe, they faid, that this murder had been committed without their confent, and efpecially fince they had taken it upon themfelves to favor thofe who committed it.

Speaking to the father of the criminal, they reprefented to him the enormity of the deed committed by his fon, faying that as reparation for it he deferved death, fince by our law fo wicked a deed did not go unpunifhed, and that whoever was found guilty and convicted of it deferved to be condemned to death as reparation for fo heinous an act; but, as to the other inhabitants of the country, who were not guilty of the crime, they faid no one wifhed them any harm or defired to vifit upon them the confequences of it.

All the favages, having clearly heard this, faid, as their only excufe, but with all refpect, that they had not confented to this act; that they knew very well that thefe two criminals ought to be put to death, unlefs we fhould be difpofed to pardon them; that they were well aware of their wickednefs, not
before

before but after the commiſſion of the deed; that they had
been informed of the death of the two ill-fated men too late
to prevent it. Moreover, they ſaid that they had kept it
ſecret, in order to preſerve conſtantly an intimate relation-
ſhip and confidence with us, and declared that they had
adminiſtered to the evil-doers ſevere reprimands, and ſet
forth the calamity which they had not only brought upon
themſelves, but upon all their tribe, relatives and friends;
and they promiſed that ſuch a calamity ſhould never occur
again and begged us to forget this offence, and not viſit it
with the conſequences it deſerved, but rather go back to the
primary motive which induced the two ſavages to go there,
and have regard for that. Furthermore they ſaid that the
culprit had come freely and delivered himſelf into our hands,
not to be puniſhed but to receive mercy from the French.

But the father, turning to the friar,[230] ſaid with tears,
there is my ſon, who committed the ſuppoſed crime; he is
worthleſs, but conſider that he is a young, fooliſh, and incon-
ſiderate perſon, who has committed this act through paſſion,
impelled by vengeance rather than by premeditation: it is
in your power to give him life or death; you can do with
him what you pleaſe, ſince we are both in your hands.

After this addreſs, the culprit ſon, preſenting himſelf with
aſſurance, ſpoke theſe words. Fear has not ſo ſeized my
heart as to prevent my coming to receive death according
to my deſerts and your law, of which I acknowledge myſelf
guilty. Then he ſtated to the company the cauſe of the
murder, and the planning and execution of it, juſt as I have
related and here ſet forth.
                                                    After

[230] Probably Père le Caron, who was in charge of the miſſion at Quebec at
that time.

After his recital he addreffed himfelf to one of the agents and clerks of the merchants of our Affociation, named *Beauchaine*, begging him to put him to death without further formality.

Then the holy Fathers fpoke, and faid to them, that the French were not accuftomed to put their fellow-men to death fo fuddenly, and that it was neceffary **to** have a confultation with all the men of the fettlement, and **bring** forward this affair as the fubject of confideration. **This being a** matter of great confequence, it was decided that **it fhould be** carefully conducted and that it was beft to poftpone **it** to **a** more favorable occafion, which would be better adapted to obtain the truth, the prefent time not being favorable for many reafons.

In the firft place, we were weak in numbers in comparifon with the favages without and within our fettlement, who, refentful and full of vengeance as they are, would have been capable of fetting fire on all fides and creating diforder among us. In the fecond place, there would have been perpetual diftruft, and no fecurity in our intercourfe with them. In the third place, trade would have been injured, and the fervice of the King impeded.

In view of thefe and other urgent confiderations, it was decided that we ought to be contented with their putting themfelves in our power and their willingnefs to give fatisfaction fubmiffively, the father of the criminal on the one hand prefenting and offering him to the company, and he, for his part, offering to give up his own life as reftitution for his offence, juft as his father offered to produce him whenever he might be required.

This

This it was thought neceſſary to regard as a ſort of honor-
able amend, and a ſatisfaction to juſtice.   And it was conſid-
ered that if we thus pardoned the offence, not only would
the criminal receive his life from us, but, alſo, his father and
companions would feel under great obligations.   It was
thought proper, however, to ſay to them as an explanation of
our action, that, in view of the fact of the criminal's public
aſſurance that all the other ſavages were in no reſpect accomplices, or to blame for the act, and had had no knowledge of it before its accompliſhment, and in view of the fact
that he had freely offered himſelf to death, it had been decided to reſtore him to his father, who ſhould remain under
obligations to produce him at any time.   On theſe terms and
on condition that he ſhould in future render ſervice to the
French, his life was ſpared, that he and all the ſavages might
continue friends and helpers of the French.

Thus it was decided to arrange the matter until the veſſels
ſhould return from France, when, in accordance with the
opinion of the captains and others, a definite and more
authoritative ſettlement **was to be concluded**.   In the mean
time we promiſed them every favor and the preſervation of
their lives, ſaying to them, however, for our ſecurity, that
they ſhould leave ſome of their children as a kind of hoſtage,
to which they very willingly acceded, and left at the ſettlement two in the hands of the holy Fathers, who proceeded to
teach them their letters, and in leſs than three months taught
them the alphabet and how to make the letters.

From this it may be ſeen that they are capable of inſtruc-
tion and are eaſily taught, as Father Joſeph [211] can teſtify.

The

[211] *Vide Hiſtoire du Canada*, par Sagard, 1636, Vol. I. p. 45.

The veffels having fafely arrived, Sieur du Pont Gravé, fome others, and myfelf were informed how the affair had taken place, as has been narrated above, when we all decided that it was defirable to make the favages feel the enormity of this murder, but not to execute punifh-ment upon them, for various good reafons hereafter to be mentioned.

As foon as our veffels had entered the harbor of Tadouf-fac, even on the morning of the next day,[212] Sieur **du** Pont Gravé and myfelf fet fail again, on a fmall barque **of ten** or twelve tons' burden. So alfo Sieur de la Mothe, together with Father Jean d'Albeau,[213] a friar, and one of the clerks and agent of the merchants, named *Loquin,* embarked on a little fhallop, and we fet out together from Tadouffac. There remained on the veffel another friar, called Father *Modefte,*[214] together with the pilot and mafter, to take care of her. We arrived at Quebec, the place of our fettlement, on the 27th of June following. Here we found Fathers Jofeph, Paul, and Pafifique, the friars,[215] and Sieur Hebert [216] with his family, together with the other members of the fettlement.

[212] They arrived on St. John's day, *antea, note* 205, and confequently this was the 25th of June, 1618.

[213] Jean d'Olbeau.

[214] Frère Modefte Guines. *Vide Hiftoire du Canada,* par Sagard, à Paris, 1636, Vol. I. p. 40.

[215] Jofeph le Caron, Paul Huet, and Pacifique du Pleffis.

[216] Louis Hébert, an apothecary, fettled at Port Royal in La Cadie or Nova Scotia, under Poutrincourt, was there when, in 1613, poffeffion was taken in the name of Madame de Guercheville. He afterward took up his abode at Quebec with his family, probably in the year 1617. His eldeft daughter Anne was married at Quebec to Eftienne Jonqueft, a Norman, which was the firft marriage that took place with the ceremonies of the Church in Canada. His daughter Guillemette married William Couillard, and to her Champlain committed the two Indian girls, whom he was not permitted by Kirke to take with him to France, when Quebec was captured by the Englifh in 1629. Louis Hébert died at Quebec on the 25th of January, 1627. *Hiftoire du Canada,* Vol. I. pp. 41, 391.

fettlement. They were all well, and delighted at our return in good health like themfelves, through the mercy of God.

The fame day Sieur du Pont Gravé determined to go to Trois Rivières, where the merchants carried on their trading, and to take with him fome merchandife, with the purpofe of meeting Sieur des Chefnes, who was already there. He alfo took with him Loquin, as before mentioned. I ftayed at our fettlement fome days, occupying myfelf with bufinefs relating to it; among other things in building a furnace for making an experiment with certain afhes, directions for which had been given me, and which are in truth of great value; but it requires labor, diligence, watchfulnefs and fkill; and for the working of thefe afhes a fufficient number of men are needed who are acquainted with this art. This firft experiment did not prove fuccefsful, and we poftponed further trial to a more favorable opportunity.

I vifited the cultivated lands,²¹⁷ which I found planted with fine grain. The gardens contained all kinds of plants, cabbages, radifhes, lettuce, purflain, forrel, parfley, and other plants, fquafhes, cucumbers, melons, peas, beans and other vegetables, which were as fine and forward as in France. There were alfo the vines, which had been tranfplanted, already well advanced. In a word, you could fee everything growing and flourifhing. Afide from God, we are not to give the praife for this to the laborers or their fkill, for it is probable that not much is due to them, but to the richnefs and excellence of the foil, which is naturally good and adapted

---

²¹⁷ Thefe fields were doubtlefs thofe of Louis Hébert, who was the firft that came into the country with his family to live by the cultivation of the foil.

adapted for everything, as experience fhows, and might be turned to good account, not only for purpofes of tillage **and** the cultivation of fruit-trees and vines, but alfo for the nourifhment and rearing of cattle and fowl, fuch as are common in France. But the thing lacking is zeal and affeftion for the welfare and fervice of the King.

I tarried fome time at Quebec, in expeftation of further intelligence, when there arrived a barque from Tadouffac, which had been fent by Sieur du Pont Gravé to get the men and merchandife remaining at that place on the beforementioned large veffel. Leaving Quebec, I embarked with them for Trois Rivières, where the trading was going on, in order to fee the favages and communicate with them, and afcertain what was taking place refpecting the affaffination above fet forth, and what could be done to fettle and fmooth over the whole matter.

On the 5th of July following I fet out from Quebec, together with Sieur de la Mothe, for Trois Rivières, both for engaging in traffic and to fee the favages. We arrived at evening off Sainte Croix,²¹⁸ a place on the way fo called. Here we faw a fhallop coming ftraight to us, in which were fome men from Sieurs du Pont Gravé and des Chefnes, and alfo fome clerks and agents of the merchants. They afked me to defpatch at once this fhallop to Quebec for fome merchandife remaining there, faying that a large number of favages had come for the purpofe of making war.

This intelligence was very agreeable to us, and in order to fatisfy them, on the morning of the next day I left my barque

²¹⁸ Platon. *Vide* Vol. I., note 155.

barque and went on board a fhallop in order to go more
fpeedily to the favages, while the other, which had come
from Trois Rivières, continued its courfe to Quebec. We
made fuch progrefs by rowing that we arrived at the before-
mentioned place on the 7th of July at 3 o'clock in the after-
noon. Upon landing, all the favages with whom I had been
intimate in their country recognized me. They were awaiting me with impatience, and came up to me very happy and
delighted to fee me again, one after the other embracing me
with demonftrations of great joy, I alfo receiving them in
the fame manner. In this agreeable way was fpent the
evening and remainder of this day, and on the next day
the favages held a council among themfelves, to afcertain
from me whether I would again affift them, as I had done
in the paft and as I had promifed them, in their wars againft
their enemies, by whom they are cruelly haraffed and tortured.

Meanwhile on our part we took counfel together to determine what we fhould do in the matter of the murder of the
two deceafed, in order that juftice might be done, and that
they might be reftrained from committing fuch an offence
in future.

In regard to the affiftance urgently requefted by the favages for making war againft their enemies, I replied that
my difpofition had not changed nor my courage abated, but
that what prevented me from affifting them was that on the
previous year, when the occafion and opportunity prefented,
they failed me when the time came; becaufe when they had
promifed to return with a good number of warriors they did
not do fo, which caufed me to withdraw without accomplifhing much. Yet I told them the matter fhould be taken into
                                        confideration.

confideration, but that for the prefent it was proper to **deter-**
mine what fhould be done in regard to the affaffination **of**
the two unfortunate men, and that fatisfaction muft be had.
Upon this they left their council in feeming anger and vex-
ation about the matter, offering to kill the criminals, and
proceed at once to their execution, if affent were given, and
acknowledging freely among themfelves the enormity of the
affair.

But we would not confent to this, poftponing **our affift-**
ance to another time, requiring them to return to us **the**
next year with a good number of men. **I affured them,**
moreover, that I would entreat the King to favor us with
men, means, and fupplies to affift them and enable them
to enjoy the reft they longed for, and victory over their enemies. At this they were greatly pleafed, and thus we
feparated, after they had held two or three meetings on the
fubject, cofting us feveral hours of time. Two or three
days after my arrival at this place they proceeded to make
merry, dance, and celebrate many great banquets in view
of the future war in which I was to affift them.

Then I ftated to Sieur du Pont Gravé what I thought
about this murder; that it was defirable to make a greater
demand upon them; that at prefent the favages would dare
not only to do the fame thing again but what would be more
injurious to us; that I confidered them people who were
governed by example; that they might accufe the French
of being wanting in courage; that if we faid no more about
the matter they would infer that we were afraid of them:
and that if we fhould let them go fo eafily they would
grow more infolent, bold, and intolerable, and we fhould even
thereby

thereby tempt them to undertake greater and more pernicious defigns. Moreover I faid that the other tribes of favages, who had or fhould get knowledge of this act, and that it had been unrevenged, or compromifed by gifts and prefents, as is their cuftom, would boaft that killing a man is no great matter; fince the French make fo little account of feeing their companions killed by their neighbors, who drink, eat, and affociate intimately with them, as may be feen.

But, on the other hand, in confideration of the various circumftances; namely, that the favages do not exercife reafon, that they are hard to approach, are eafily eftranged, and are very ready to take vengeance, that, if we fhould force them to inflict punifhment, there would be no fecurity for thofe defirous of making explorations among them, we determined to fettle this affair in a friendly manner, and pafs over quietly what had occurred, leaving them to engage peaceably in their traffic with the clerks and agents of the merchants and others in charge.

Now there was with them a man named *Eftienne Brûlé*, one of our interpreters, who had been living with them for eight years, as well to pafs his time as to fee the country and learn their language and mode of life. He is the one whom I had defpatched with orders to go in the direction of the Entouhonorons,[219] to Carantoüan, in order to bring with

<hr/>

[219] Champlain fays, *donné charge d'aller vers les Entouhonorons à Carantouan.* By reference to the map of 1632, it will be feen that the Entouhonorons were fituated on the fouthern borders of Lake Ontario. They were underftood by Champlain to be a part at leaft of the Iroquois: but the Carantouanais, allies of the Hurons, were fouth of them, occupying apparently the upper waters of the Sufquehanna. A dotted line will be feen on the fame map, evidently intended to mark the courfe of Brûlé's journey. From the meagre knowledge which Champlain poffeffed of the region, the line

with him the five hundred warriors they had promifed
to fend to affift us in the war in which we were engaged
againft their enemies, a reference to which is made in the
narrative of my previous book.[220]   I called this man, namely
Etienne Brûlé, and afked him why he had not brought the
affiftance of the five hundred men, and what was the caufe
of the delay, and why he had not rendered me a report.
Thereupon he gave me an account of the matter, a narrative of which it will not be out of place to give, as he **is more**
to be pitied than blamed on account of the misfortunes which
he experienced on this commiffion.

He proceeded to fay that, after taking leave of me to go
on his journey and execute his commiffion, he fet out with
the twelve favages whom I had given him for the purpofe
of fhowing the way, and to ferve as an efcort on account of
the dangers which he might have to encounter.   They were
fuccefsful in reaching the place, Carantouan, but not without expofing themfelves to rifk, fince they had to pafs
through the territories of their enemies, and, in order to
avoid any evil defign, purfued a more fecure route through
thick and impenetrable forefts, wood and brufh, marfhy bogs,
frightful and unfrequented places and waftes, all to avoid
danger and a meeting with their enemies.

But, in fpite of this great care, Brûlé and his favage
companions, while croffing a plain, encountered fome hoftile
favages,

fhe can hardly be fuppofed to be very
accurate, which may account for Champlain's indefinite expreffion as cited at
the beginning of this note.

The Entouhonorons, Ouentouoro-
nons, Tfonnontouans, or Senecas con-
ftituted the moft weftern and moft numerous canton of the Five Nations.
*Vide Continuation of the New Difcov-
ery,* by Louis Hennepin, 1699, p. 93;
also Origin of the name Seneca in Mr.
O. H. Marfhall's brochure on *De la
Salle among the Senecas,* pp. 43–45.
[220] *Vide antea,* p. 124.

favages, who were returning to their village and who were furprifed and worfted by our favages, four of the enemy being killed on the fpot and two taken prifoners, whom Brûlé and his companions took to Carantoüan, by the inhabitants of which place they were received with great affection, a cordial welcome, and good cheer, with the dances and banquets with which they are accuftomed to entertain and honor ftrangers.

Some days were fpent in this friendly reception ; and, after Brûlé had told them his miffion and explained to them the occafion of his journey, the favages of the place affembled in council to deliberate and refolve in regard to fending the five hundred warriors afked for by Brûlé.

When the council was ended and it was decided to fend the men, orders were given to collect, prepare, and arm them, fo as to go and join us where we were encamped before the fort and village of our enemies. This was only three fhort days' journey from Carantoüan, which was provided with more than eight hundred warriors, and ftrongly fortified, after the manner of thofe before defcribed, which have high and ftrong palifades well bound and joined together, the quarters being conftructed in a fimilar fafhion.

After it had been refolved by the inhabitants of Carantoüan to fend the five hundred men, thefe were very long in getting ready, although urged by Brûlé, to make hafte, who explained to them that if they delayed any longer they would **not find us** there. And in fact they did not fucceed in arriving until two days after our departure from that place, which we were forced to abandon, fince we were too weak and worn by the inclemency of the weather. This

caufed

caufed Brûlé, and the five hundred men whom he brought, to withdraw and return to their village of Carantoüan. After their return Brûlé was obliged to ftay, and fpend the reft of the autumn and all the winter, for lack of company and efcort home. While awaiting, he bufied himfelf in exploring the country and vifiting the tribes and territories adjacent to that place, and in making a tour along **a** river [221] that debouches in the direction of Florida, where are many powerful and warlike nations, carrying on **wars** againft each other. The climate there is very temperate, and there are great numbers of animals and abundance of fmall game. But to traverfe and reach thefe regions requires patience, on account of the difficulties involved in paffing the extenfive waftes.

He continued his courfe along the river as far as the fea, [222] and to iflands and lands near them, which are inhabited by various tribes and large numbers of favages, who are well difpofed and love the French above all other nations. But thofe who know the Dutch [223] complain feverely of them, fince they treat them very roughly. Among other things he obferved that the winter was very temperate, that it fnowed very rarely, and that when it did the fnow was not a foot deep and melted immediately.

After traverfing the country and obferving what was noteworthy, he returned to the village of Carantoüan, in order to find an efcort for returning to our fettlement. After fome

ftay

[221] The River Sufquehanna.　[222] He appears to have gone as far fouth at leaft as the upper waters of Chefapeake Bay.　[223] The Dutch fur-traders. *Vide Hiftory of the State of New York* by John Romeyn Brodhead, Vol. I. p. 44 *et paffim.*

ſtay at Carantoüan, five or ſix of the ſavages decided to make
the journey with Brûlé. On the way they encountered a
large number of their enemies, who charged upon Brûlé and
his companions ſo violently that they cauſed them to break
up and ſeparate from each other, ſo that they were unable
to rally: and Brûlé, who had kept apart in the hope of
eſcaping, became ſo detached from the others that he could
not return, nor find a road or ſign in order to effect his
retreat in any direction whatever. Thus he continued to
wander through foreſt and wood for ſeveral days without
eating, and almoſt deſpairing of his life from the preſſure
of hunger. At laſt he came upon a little footpath, which he
determined to follow wherever it might lead, whether toward
the enemy or not, preferring to expoſe himſelf to their hands
truſting in God rather than to die alone and in this wretched
manner. Beſides he knew how to ſpeak their language,
which he thought might afford him ſome aſſiſtance.

But he had not gone a long diſtance when he diſcovered
three ſavages loaded with fiſh repairing to their village. He
ran after them, and, as he approached, ſhouted at them, as
is their cuſtom. At this they turned about, and filled with
fear were about to leave their burden and flee. But Brûlé
ſpeaking to them reaſſured them, when they laid down their
bows and arrows in ſign of peace, Brûlé on his part laying
down his arms. Moreover he was weak and feeble, not having eaten for three or four days. On coming up to them,
after he had told them of his misfortune and the miſerable
condition to which he had been reduced, they ſmoked together, as they are accuſtomed to do with one another and
their acquaintances **when they viſit each other.** They had
pity

pity and compaſſion for him, offering him every aſſiſtance, and conducting him to their village, where they entertained him and gave him ſomething to eat.

But as ſoon as the people of the place were informed that an *Adoreſetoüy* had arrived, for thus they call the French, the name ſignifying *men of iron*, they came in a ruſh and in great numbers to ſee Brûlé. They took him to the cabin of one of the principal chiefs, where he was interrogated, and aſked who he **was**, whence **he came**, what circumſtance had driven and led him to this place, **how** he had loſt his way, and whether he did not belong to the French nation that made war upon them. To this he replied that he belonged to a better nation, that was deſirous ſolely of their acquaintance and friendſhip. Yet they would not believe this, but threw themſelves upon him, tore out his nails with their teeth, burnt him with glowing firebrands, and tore out his beard, hair by hair, though contrary to the will of the chief.

During this fit of paſſion, one of the ſavages obſerved an *Agnus Dei*, which he had attached to his neck, and aſked what it was that he had thus attached to his neck, and was on the point of ſeizing it and pulling it off. But Brûlé ſaid to him, with reſolute words, If you take it and put me to death, you will find that immediately after you will ſuddenly die, and all thoſe of your houſe. He paid no attention however to this, but continuing in his malicious purpoſe tried to ſeize the *Agnus Dei* and tear it from him, all of them together being deſirous of putting him to death, but previouſly of making him ſuffer great pain and torture, ſuch as they generally practiſe upon their enemies.

But

But God, fhowing him mercy, was pleafed not to allow it, but in his providence caufed the heavens to change fuddenly from the ferene and fair ftate they were in to darknefs, and to become filled with great and thick clouds, upon **which** followed thunders and lightnings fo violent and long continued that it was fomething ftrange and awful. This ftorm caufed the favages fuch terror, it being not only unufual but unlike anything they had ever heard, that their attention was diverted and they forgot the evil purpofe they had towards Brûlé, their prifoner. They accordingly left him without even unbinding him, as they did not dare to approach him. This gave the fufferer an opportunity to ufe gentle words, and he appealed to them and remonftrated with them on the harm they were doing him without caufe, and fet forth to them how our God was enraged at them for having fo abufed him.

The captain then approached Brûlé, unbound him, and took **him** to his houfe, where he took care of him and treated his wounds. After this there were no dances, banquets, or merry-makings to which Brûlé was not invited. So after remaining fome time with thefe favages, he determined to proceed towards our fettlement.

Taking leave of them, he promifed to reftore them to harmony with the French and their enemies, and caufe them to fwear friendfhip with each other, to which end he faid he would return to them as foon as he could. Thence he went **to** the **country** and village of the Atinouaentans,[224] where I

had

---

[224] Attigouantans or Attignaouantans. The principal tribe of the Hurons, fometimes called *Les bons Iroquois*, as they and the Iroquois were of the fame original ftock. *Vide* Vol. I. p. 276, note 212.

had already been; the favages at his departure having conducted him for a diftance of four days' journey from their
village. Here Brûlé remained fome time, when, refuming
his journey towards us he came by way of the Mer Douce,²⁸⁵
boating along its northern fhores for fome ten days, where
I had alfo gone when on my way to the war.

And if Brûlé had gone further on to explore thefe regions, as I had directed him to do, it would not have been
a mere rumor that they were preparing war with one another. But this undertaking was referved to another time,
which he promifed me to continue and accomplifh in a fhort
period with God's grace, and to conduct me there that I
might obtain fuller and more particular knowledge.

After he had made this recital, I gave him affurance that
his fervices would be recognized, and encouraged him to
continue his good purpofe until our return, when we fhould
have more abundant means to do that with which he would
be fatisfied. This is now the entire narrative and recital of
his journey from the time he left me²⁸⁶ to engage in the
above-mentioned

²⁸⁵ Lake Huron. For the different
names which have been attached to this
lake, *vide Local Names of Niagara
Frontier,* by Orfamus H. Marfhall, 1881,
p. 37.

²⁸⁶ Brûlé was defpatched on his miffion Sept. 8, 1615. *Vide antes.* p. 124.

As we have already ftated in a previous note, it was the policy of Champlain to place competent young men with
the different tribes of favages, to obtain
that kind of information which could
only come from an actual and prolonged
refidence with them. This enabled him
to fecure not only the moft accurate
knowledge of their domeftic habits and
cuftoms, the character and fpirit of their
life, but thefe young men by their long
refidence with the favages acquired a
good knowledge of their language, and
were able to act as interpreters. This
was a matter of very great importance,
as it was often neceffary for Champlain
to communicate with the different tribes
in making treaties of friendfhip, in difcuff-
ing queftions of war with their enemies,
in fettling difagreements among themfelves, and in making arrangements with
them for the yearly purchafe of their
peltry. It was not eafy to obtain fuitable perfons for this important office.
Thofe who had the intellectual qualifi-
cations.

above-mentioned explorations; and it afforded me pleafure in the profpect thereby prefented me of being better able to continue and promote them.

With this purpofe he took leave of me to return to the favages, an intimate acquaintance with whom had been acquired by him in his journeys and explorations. I begged him to continue with them until the next year, when I would return with a good number of men, both to reward him for his labors, and to affift as in the paft the favages, his friends, in their wars.

Refuming the thread of my former difcourfe, I muft note that in my laft and preceding voyages and explorations I had paffed through numerous and diverfe tribes of favages

not

cations, and who had any high afpirations, would not naturally incline to pafs years in the ftupid and degrading affociations, to fay nothing of the hardfhips and deprivations, of favage life. They were generally therefore adventurers, whofe honefty and fidelity had no better foundation than their felfifh interefts. Of this fort was this Étienne Brûlé, as well as Nicholas Marfolet and Pierre Raye, all of whom turned traitors, felling themfelves to the Englifh when Quebec was taken in 1629. Of Brûlé, Champlain ufes the following emphatic language: "Le truchement Bruflé à qui l'on donnoit cent piftolles par an, pour inciter les fauvages à venir à la traitte, ce qui eftoit de tref-mauvais exemple, d'envoyer ainfi des perfonnes fi mahuluans, que l'on euft deub chaftier feuerement, car l'on recognoifloit cet homme pour eftre fort vicieux, & adonné aux femmes; mais que ne fait faire l'efperance du gain, qui paffe par deffus toutes confiderations." *Vide iffue of* 1632, Quebec ed., pp. 1065, 1229.

But among Champlain's interpreters there were doubtlefs fome who bore a very different character. Jean Nicolet was certainly a marked exception. Although Champlain does not mention him by name, he appears to have been in New France as early as 1618, where he fpent many years among the Algonquins, and was the firft Frenchman who penetrated the diftant Northweft. He married into one of the moft refpectable families of Quebec, and is often mentioned in the Relations des Jéfuites. *Vide* a brief notice of him in *Difcovery and Exploration of the Miffiffippi Valley*, by John Gilmary Shea, 1852, p. xx. A full account of his career has recently been publifhed, entitled *Hiftory of the Difcovery of the Northweft by John Nicolet in 1634, with a Sketch of his Life*. By C. W. Butterfield. Cincinnati, 1881. *Vide alfo Détails fur la Vie de Jean Nicollet*, an extract from *Relation des Jéfuites*, 1643, in *Découvertes, etc.*, par Pierre Margry, p. 49.

not known to the French nor to thofe of our fettlement, with whom I had made alliances and fworn friendfhip, on condition that they fhould come and trade with us, and that I fhould affift them in their wars; for it muft be underftood that there is not a fingle tribe living in peace, excepting the Nation Neutre. According to their promife, there came from the various tribes of favages recently difcovered fome to trade in peltry, others to fee the French and afcertain what kind of treatment and welcome **would be** fhown **them.** This encouraged everybody, the French on the one hand to fhow them cordiality and welcome, for they honored them with fome attentions and prefents, which the agents of **the** merchants gave to gratify them; on the other hand, it **en-**couraged the favages, who promifed all the French to come and live in future in friendfhip with them, all of them declaring that they would deport themfelves with fuch affection towards us that we fhould have occafion to commend them, while we in like manner were to affift them to the extent of our power in their wars.

The trading having been concluded, and the favages having taken their leave and departed, we left Trois Rivières on the 14th of July of this year. The next day we arrived at our quarters at Quebec, where the barques were unloaded of the merchandife which had remained over from the traffic and which was put in the warehoufe of the **mer-**chants at that place.

Now Sieur de Pont Gravé went to Tadouffac with the barques in order to load them and carry to the habitation the provifions neceffary to fupport thofe who were to remain and winter there, and I determined while the barques were thus

thus engaged to continue there for some days in order to have the necessary fortifications and repairs made.

At my departure from the settlement I took leave of the holy Fathers, Sieur de la Mothe, and all the others who were to stay there, giving them to expect that I would return, God assisting, with a good number of families to people the country. I embarked on the 26th of July, together with the Fathers Paul and Pacifique,[297] the latter having wintered here once and the other having been here a year and a half, who were to make a report of what they had seen in the country and of what could be done there. We set out on the day above mentioned from the settlement for Tadoussac, where we were to embark for France. We arrived the next day and found our vessels ready to set sail. We embarked, and left Tadoussac for France on the 13th of the month of July, 1618, and arrived at Honfleur on the 28th day of August, the wind having been favorable, and all being in good spirits.

[297] Paul Huet and Pacifique du Plessis. The latter had been in New France more than a year and a half, having arrived in 1615. *Vide antea*, pp. 104-5.

EXPLANATION

OF

TWO GEOGRAPHICAL MAPS OF NEW FRANCE.

T has feemed to me well to make fome ftatements in explanation of the two geographical
maps. Although one correfponds to the other
fo far as the harbors, bays, capes, promonto-
ries, and rivers extending into the interior are
concerned, neverthelefs they are different in refpect to the
bearings.

The fmalleft is in its true meridian, in accordance with
the directions of Sieur de Caftelfranc in his book on the
mecometry of the magnetic needle,[228] where I have noted,
as will be feen on the map, feveral declinations, which have
been

---

[228] The determination of longitudes
has from the beginning been environed
with almoft infuperable difficulties. At
one period the declination of the magnetic needle was fuppofed to furnifh the
means of a practical folution. Sebaf-
tian Cabot devoted confiderable attention to the fubject, as did likewife Peter
Plancius at a later date. Champlain
appears to have fixed the longitudes on
his fmaller map by calculations bafed
on the variation of the needle, guided
by the principles laid down by Guil-
laume de Nautonier, Sieur de Caftelfranc, to whofe work he refers in the
text. It was entitled, *Mécométrie de
l'eymant, c'eft à dire la maniere de me-
furer les longitudes par le moyen de
l'eymant.*

been of much fervice to me, fo alfo all the altitudes, latitudes, and longitudes, from the forty-firft degree of latitude to the fifty-firft, in the direction of the North Pole, which are the **confines of Canada, or the Great** Bay, where more efpecially **the Bafques and** Spaniards engage in the whale fifhery. In certain places in the great river St. Lawrence, in latitude 45°, I have obferved the declination of the magnetic needle, and found it as high as twenty-one degrees, which is the greateft I have feen.

The fmall map will ferve very well for purpofes of navigation, provided the needle be applied properly to the rofe [290] indicating the points of the compafs. For inftance, in ufing it, when one is on the Grand Bank where frefh fifhing is carried on, it is neceffary, for the fake of greater convenience, to take a rofe where the thirty-two points are marked equally, and put the point of the magnetic needle 12, 15, or 16 degrees from the *fleur de lis* on the northweft fide, **which** is nearly a point and a half, that is north a point northweft,

Fermont. This rare volume is not to be found, as far as my inquiries extend, in any of the incorporated libraries on this continent. There is however a copy in the Bodleian Library at Oxford, to which in the catalogue is given the bibliographical note: *Six livres. Folio. Tolofe,* 1603.

It is hardly neceffary to add that the forces governing the variation of the needle, both local and general, are fo inconftant that the hope of fixing longitudes by it was long fince abandoned.

The reafon for the introduction of the explanation of the maps at this place will be feen *antea,* p. 39.

[290] The *rofe* is the face or card of the mariner's compafs. It was anciently called the *fly.* Card may perhaps be derived from the Italian *carda,* a thiftle, which the face of the compafs may be fuppofed to refemble. On the complete circle of the compafs there are thirty-two lines drawn from the centre to the circumference to indicate the direction of the wind. Each quarter of the circle, or 90°, contains eight lines reprefenting the points of the compafs in that quarter. They are named with reference to the cardinal points from which they begin, as 1, north; 2, north by eaft; 3, north-northeaft; 4, northeaft by north; 5, northeaft; 6, northeaft by eaft; 7, eaft-northeaft; 8, eaft by north. The points in each quarter are named in a fimilar manner.

northwest or a little more, from the *fleur de lis* of said **rose**, and then adjust the rose to the compass. By this means the latitudes of all the capes, harbors, and rivers can be accurately ascertained.

I am aware that there are many who will not make use of it, but will prefer to run according to the large one, since it is made according to the compass of France, where the magnetic needle varies to the northeast, for the reason that they are so accustomed **to this method that it is** difficult for them to change. For this reason I have prepared the large map in this manner, for the assistance **of the** majority of the pilots and mariners in the waters of New France, fearing that if I had not done so, they would have ascribed to me a mistake, not knowing whence it proceeded. For the small plans or charts of Newfoundland are, for the most part, different in all their statements with respect to the positions of the lands and their latitudes. And those who may have some small copies, reasonably good, esteem them so valuable that they do not communicate a knowledge of them to their country, which might derive profit therefrom.

Now the construction of these maps is such that they have their meridian in a direction north-northeast, making west west-northwest, which is contrary to the true meridian of this place, namely, to call north-northeast north, for the needle instead of varying to the northwest, as it should, varies to the northeast as if it were in France. The consequence of this is that error has resulted, and will continue to do so, since this antiquated custom is practised, which they still retain, although they fall into grave mistakes.

They

They also make use of a compass marked north and south; that is, so that the point of the magnetic needle is directly on the *fleur de lis*. In accordance with such a compass many construct their small maps, which seems to me the **better** way, and so approach nearer to the true meridian of **New** France, than the compasses of France proper, which point to the northeast. It has come about, consequently, in this way that the first navigators who sailed to New France thought there was no greater deviation in going to these parts than to the Azores, or other places near France, where the deviation is almost imperceptible in navigation, the navigators having the compasses of France, which point northeast and represent the true meridian. In sailing constantly westward with the purpose of reaching a certain latitude, they laid their course directly west by their compass, supposing that they were sailing on the one parallel where they wished to go. By thus going constantly in a straight line and not in a circle, as all the parallels on the surface of the globe run, they found after having traversed a long distance, and as they were approaching the land, that they were some three, four, or five degrees farther south than they ought to be, thus being deceived in their true latitude and reckoning.

It is true, indeed, that, when the weather was fair and the sun clearly visible, they corrected their latitude, but not without wondering how it happened that their course was wrong, which arose in consequence of their sailing in a straight instead of a circular line according to the parallel, so that in changing their meridian they changed with regard to the points of the compass, and consequently their course. It is, therefore,

therefore, very neceſſary to know the meridian, and **the dec-**
lination of the magnetic needle, for this knowledge can ſerve
all navigators. This is eſpecially ſo in the north and ſouth,
where there are greater variations in the magnetic needle,
and where the meridians of longitude are ſmaller, ſo that the
error, if the declination were not known, would be greater.
This above-mentioned error has accordingly ariſen, becauſe
navigators have either not cared to correct it, or did not
know how to do ſo, and **have left it in the** ſtate in which
it now is. It is conſequently difficult to abandon **this man-**
ner of ſailing in the regions of New France.

This has led me to make this large map, not only that it
might be more minute than the ſmall one, but alſo in order
to ſatisfy navigators, who will thus be able to ſail as they do
according to their ſmall maps ; and they will excuſe me for
not making it better and more in detail, for the life of a
man is not long enough to obſerve things ſo exactly that at
leaſt ſomething would not be found to have been omitted.
Hence inquiring and pains-taking perſons will, in ſailing,
obſerve things not to be found on this map, but which they
can add to it, ſo that in the courſe of time there will be no
doubt as to any of the localities indicated. At leaſt it ſeems
to me that I have done my duty, ſo far as I could, not having
failed to put on my map anything that I have ſeen, and thus
giving to the public ſpecial knowledge of what had never
been deſcribed, nor ſo carefully explored as I have done it.
Although in the paſt others have written of theſe things,
yet very little in compariſon with what we have explored
within the paſt ten years.

MODE

MODE OF DETERMINING A MERIDIAN LINE.

TAKE a small piece of board, perfectly level, and place in the middle a needle C, three inches high, so that it shall be exactly perpendicular. Expose it to the sun before noon, at 8 or 9 o'clock, and mark the point B at the end of the shadow cast by the needle. Then opening the compasses, with one point on C and the other on the shadow B, describe an arc AB. Leave the whole in this position until afternoon when you see the shadow just reaching the arc at A. Then divide equally the arc AB, and taking a rule, and placing it **on** the points C and D, draw a line running the whole length of the board, which is not to be moved until the observation is completed. This line will be the meridian of the place you are in.

And in order to ascertain the declination of the place where you are with reference to the meridian, place a compass, which must be rectangular, along the meridian line, as shown in the figure above, there being upon the card a circle divided into 360 degrees. Divide the circle by two diametrical lines; one representing the north and south, as indicated by EF, the other the east and west, as indicated by GH. Then observe the magnetic needle turning on its pivot upon the card, and you will see how much it deviates **from** the fixed meridian line upon the card, and how many degrees it varies to the northeast or northwest.

CHAMPLAIN'S

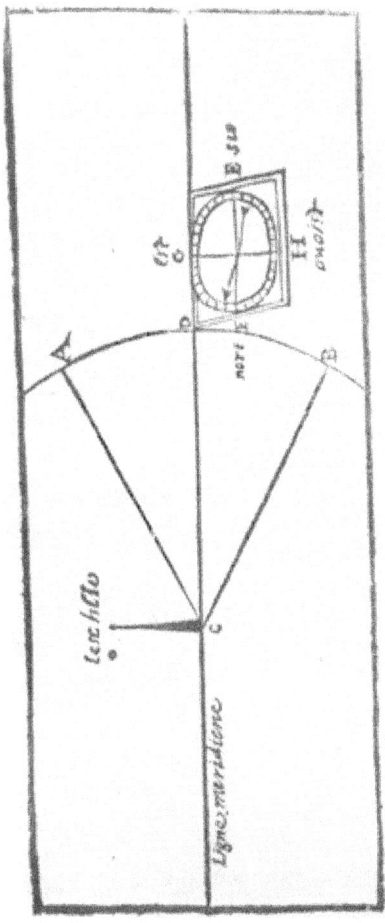

lenchtto

Ligne meridiene

O 49

E est

(nord)

H

nord

CHAMPLAIN'S LARGE MAP.

GEOGRAPHICAL CHART OF **NEW** FRANCE, MADE BY SIEUR DE CHAMPLAIN OF SAINTONGE, CAPTAIN IN ORDINARY **FOR THE** KING IN THE MARINE. MADE IN THE YEAR 1612.

HAVE made this **map for the** greater convenience of the majority **of thofe** who navigate on thefe coafts, fince **they fail to that country according to** compaffes **arranged** for the hemifphere of Afia. And **if I** had made it **like** the fmall **one,** the majority would **not have** been able to ufe it, **owing to** their not knowing the declinations of the needle.[290]

Obferve that on the prefent map north-northeaft ftands **for north,** and weft-northweft **for** weft; according to which one is to be guided in afcertaining the elevation of the degrees of latitude, as if thefe points were actually eaft and weft, north and fouth, fince the map is conftructed according to the compaffes of France, which vary to the northeaft.[291]

SOME DECLINATIONS OF THE MAGNETIC NEEDLE,
WHICH I HAVE CAREFULLY OBSERVED.

Cap Breton	14° 50'	St. Croix	17° 32'
Cap de la Hève	16° 15'	Rivière de Norumbegue	18° 40'
Baye Ste. Marie	17° 16'	Quinibequi	19° 12'
Port Royal	17° 8'	Mallebarre	18° 40'
En la grande R. St. Laurent	21°		

All obferved by Sieur de Champlain, 1612.

REFERENCES

[290] The above title is on the large map of 1612. This note is on the upper left-hand corner of the fame map.

[291] For this note fee the upper right-hand corner of the map.

29

REFERENCES ON CHAMPLAIN'S LARGE **MAP.**

A. Port Fortuné.
B. Baye Blanche.
C. Baye aux Isles.
D. Cap des Isles.
E. Port aux Isles.
F. Isle Haute.
G. Isle des Monts Déferts.
H. Cap Corneille.
I. Isles aux Oiseaux.
K. Cap des Deux Bayes.
L. Port aux Mines.
M. Cap Fourchu.
N. Cap Nègre.
O. Port du Roffignol.
P. St. Laurent.
Q. Rivière de l'Isle Verte.
R. Baye Saine.
S. Rivière Sainte Marguerite.
T. Port Sainte Hélène.
V. Isle des Martires.
X. Isles Rangées.
Y. Port de Savalette.
Z. Paffage du Glas.

1. Port aux Anglois.
2. Baye Courante.
3. Cap de Poutrincourt.
4. Isle Gravée.
5. Paffage Courant.
6. Baye de Gennes.
7. Isle Perdue.
8. Cap des Mines.
9. Port aux Coquilles.
10. Isles Jumelles.
11. Cap Saint Jean.
12. Isle la Nef.
13. La Heronnière Isle.
14. Isles Rangées.
15. Baye Saint Luc.
16. Paffage du Gas.
17. Côte de Montmorency.
18. Rivière de Champlain.
19. Rivière Sainte Marie.
20. Isle d'Orléans.
21. Isle de Bacchus.

NOTE. — The reader will obferve that in a few inftances the references are wanting on the map.

CHAMPLAIN'S

CHAMPLAIN'S NOTE TO THE SMALL MAP.

N the fmall map[299] is added the ftrait above La-brador between the fifty-third and fixty-third degrees of latitude, which the Englifh have dif-covered duing the prefent year 1612, in their voyage to find, if poffible, a paffage to China by way of the north.[300] They wintered at a place indicated by this mark, ϵ. But it was not without enduring fevere cold, and they were obliged to return to England, leaving their leader in the northern regions. Within fix months three other veffels have fet out, to penetrate, if poffible, ftill farther, and, at the fame time, to fearch for the men who were left in that region.

GEOGRAPHICAL

[299] In Champlain's iffue in 1613, the note here given was placed in the preliminary matter to that volume. It was placed there probably after the reft of the work had gone to prefs. We have placed it here in connection with other matter relating to the maps, where it feems more properly to belong.

[300] This refers to the fourth voyage of Henry Hudfon, made in 1610, for the purpofe here indicated. He penetrated Lomley's Inlet, hoping to find a paffage through to the Pacific Ocean, or, as it was then called, the South Sea, and thus find a direct and fhorter courfe to China. He paffed the winter at about 52° north latitude, in that expanfe of water which has ever fince been appropriately known as Hudfon's Bay. A mutiny having broken out among his crew, he and eight others having been forced into a fmall boat, on the 21ft of June, 1611, were fet adrift on the fea, and were never heard of afterward.

A part of the mutinous crew arrived with the fhip in England, and were immediately thrown into prifon. The following year, 1612, an expedition under Sir Thomas Button was fent out to feek for Hudfon, and to profecute the fearch ftill further for a northweft paffage. It is needlefs to add that the fearch was unfuccefsful.

A chart by Hudfon fortunately efcaped deftruction by the mutineers. Singularly enough, an engraving of it, entitled, TABVLA NAVTICA, was publifhed by Heffel Gerritz at Amfterdam the fame year. Champlain incorporated the part of it illuftrating Hudfon's difcovery in his fmaller map, which is dated the fame year, 1612. He does not introduce it into his large map, although that is dated likewife 1612. A fac-fimile of the Tabula Nautica is given in *Henry Hudfon the Navigator*, by G. M. Afher, LL.D., publifhed by the Hakluyt Society in 1860.

GEOGRAPHICAL MAP OF NEW FRANCE, IN ITS TRUE MERIDIAN.

Made by Sieur Champlain, Captain for the King in the Marine. 1613.

๐ Matou-ouefcariny. 1.	*R.* Port au Mouton.
○ Gafpay.	*S.* Port du Roffignol. 6.
∞ Ouefcariny. 2.	*SS.* Lac de Medicis. 7.
o-o Quenongebin. 3.	*T.* Sefambre.
A. Tadouffac.	*V.* Cap des Deux Bayes.
B. Lefquemain.	3. L'Ifle aux Coudres.
C. Ifle Percée.	4. Saincte Croix. 8.
D. Baye de Chaleur.	4. Rivière des Etechemins. 9.
E. Ifles aux Gros Yeux. 4.	5. Sault. 10.
H. Baye Françoife.	6. Lac Sainct Pierre.
I. Ifles aux Oyfeaux.	7. Rivière des Yroquois.
L. Rivière des Etechemins. 5.	9. Ifle aux Lieures.
M. Menane.	10. Rivière Platte. 11.
N. Port Royal.	11. Mantane. 12.
P. Ifle Longue.	40. Cap Saincte Marie. 13.
Q. Cap Fourchu.	

1. This figure is inverted on the map. *Vide antea,* note 59, p. 62 2. *Vide antea,* note 47, pp. 59, 81. The figure ∞ is mifplaced and fhould be where o-o is on the map, on the extreme weftern border near the forty-feventh degree of north latitude. 3. This figure o-o on the map occupies the place which fhould be occupied by ∞. *Vide antea,* p. 58, note 46. 4. A clufter of iflands of which the ifland of Birds is one. 5. This letter, placed between the River St. John and the St. Croix, refers to the latter. 6. The letter S appears twice on the coaft of La Cadie. The one here referred to is the more wefterly. 7. This reference is probably to the Lake of Two Mountains, which will be feen on the map weft of Montreal. 8. St. Croix on the map is where a crofs furmounted by the figure 4 may be feen. 9. This appears to refer to the Chaudière. *Vide* Vol. I. p. 296. 10. This refers to the Falls of Montmorency. 11. A fmall river flowing into Mal Bay. *Vide* Vol. I. p. 295; alfo *Les Voyages de Champlain,* Quebec ed., p. 1069. 12. *Vide* Vol. I. p. 234. 13. The figures are wanting. Cape St. Mary is on the fouthern coaft of Newfoundland. *Vide* Vol. I. p. 232.

INDEX.

INDEX.

www.ingramcontent.com/pod-product-compliance
Lightning Source LLC
Chambersburg PA
CBHW030352270326

41926CB00009B/1075